Praise for *Stepping up*

▐▐ Sarah is one of the most inspiring leaders I know; anyone wanting to become one too should read this book.

BARONESS MARTHA LANE FOX, FOUNDER, LASTMINUTE.COM; CHANCELLOR, THE OPEN UNIVERSITY; BOARD MEMBER, TWITTER

▐▐ This book is so needed. A manual for the leadership generation that want to create their own future.

KATHRYN PARSONS, CO-FOUNDER AND CO-CEO, DECODED

▐▐ In the past, it took decades to climb up the ranks of organisations before people had a shot at being a leader. Today, leadership can be practised at all levels. Sarah Wood argues this is not only possible but desirable. We all should step up or step out of the way for others.

THALES TEIXEIRA, PROFESSOR, HARVARD UNIVERSITY

Stepping up

Stepping up

How to accelerate your leadership potential

Sarah Wood

Niamh O'Keeffe

Pearson

Harlow, England • London • New York • Boston • San Francisco • Toronto • Sydney • Dubai • Singapore • Hong Kong
Tokyo • Seoul • Taipei • New Delhi • Cape Town • São Paulo • Mexico City • Madrid • Amsterdam • Munich • Paris • Milan

PEARSON EDUCATION LIMITED
KAO Two
KAO Park
Harlow CM17 9NA
United Kingdom
Tel: +44 (0)1279 623623
Web: www.pearson.com/uk

First edition published 2018 (print and electronic)
© Pearson Education Limited 2018 (print and electronic)

The rights of Sarah Wood and Niamh O'Keeffe to be identified as authors of this work have been asserted by them in accordance with the Copyright, Designs and Patents Act 1988.

ISBN: 978-1-292-18642-9 (print)
      978-1-292-18687-0 (PDF)
      978-1-292-18688-7 (ePub)

British Library Cataloguing-in-Publication Data
A catalogue record for the print edition is available from the British Library

Library of Congress Cataloging-in-Publication Data
A catalog record for the print edition is available from the Library of Congress

10 9 8 7 6 5 4 3 2 1
21 20 19 18 17

Cover design by Two Associates

Print edition typeset in 10.25pt Frutiger LT Com by SPi Global
Print edition printed and bound in the UK by Ashford Colour Press Ltd, Gosport, Hants

NOTE THAT ANY PAGE CROSS REFERENCES REFER TO THE PRINT EDITION

You're off to Great Places!
Today is your day!
Your mountain is waiting,
So . . . get on your way!

DR SEUSS, *OH, THE PLACES YOU'LL GO!*

Contents

About the authors

We are very pleased to be joining forces and collaborating on a book to help you dare to step up and fulfil your leadership potential. Sarah is a founder and Chief Executive who leads a global team in the quest to transform digital advertising for the better and believes that business culture can be a powerful agent for positive change. Niamh is a leadership consultant and adviser with experience of working with CEOs and senior leaders from a range of industries.

Sarah Wood is the co-founder and CEO of Unruly (www.unruly. co). Based in London's Tech City and led by Sarah and co-founders Scott Button and Matt Cooke, Unruly is one of the world's most innovative advertising technology companies, getting videos seen, shared and loved across the open web. Its proprietary technology brings emotional intelligence to digital advertising in order to increase viewer engagement, brand performance and publisher revenues.

Driven by an interest in the creative and collaborative opportunities afforded by the social web and internet culture, Sarah, Scott and Matt could see that online video was about to pop. Together, they successfully developed the company, opening 20 offices and working with 90 per cent of Ad Age 100 brands before selling to News Corporation in 2015 for £114 million. Unruly now employs over 300 people globally, who step up every day to #DeliverWow for brands and agencies.

Sarah is an associate lecturer at the University of Cambridge, convening and teaching an MPhil course in online video culture since 2012. From 2014 to 2016, in collaboration with Cass Business School, Unruly hosted a pop-up university offering free lectures and workshops by business leaders and academic tutors to inspire the next generation of entrepreneurs in East London's Tech City. In 2016, Sarah was awarded an honorary doctorate by City University for services to entrepreneurship.

Sarah was awarded City A.M. Entrepreneur of the Year in 2015, and CEO of the Year at TechCrunch's Europas Awards in 2016. Sarah was also awarded the prestigious title of Veuve Clicquot Business Woman of the Year in 2016. Alongside her co-founder Scott Button, Sarah was awarded an OBE for services to innovation and technology in 2016.

Niamh O'Keeffe is leadership adviser, published author and founder of First100 'a and CEOassist'. Niamh provides advice on key moments in the leadership role lifecycle: how to get promoted, how to have a great first 100 days, how to stay the course and legacy projects.

Niamh is the founder and Managing Director of First100 – a niche advisory business supporting leaders in the first 100 days of a new role appointment. She has a track record of over twenty-five years' career experience, including eight years as a strategy consultant with Accenture, two years as an executive search consultant in the City of London, and over twelve years, advisory experience as founder and Managing Director of First100 www.First100assist.com

Niamh's client list spans industries and includes advising leaders of entrepreneurial ventures as well as senior executives at global corporations like Accenture, Microsoft and Oliver Wyman Group.

Niamh is a three-time published Pearson author, and her FT Publishing International titles include:

- *Your First 100 Days: how to make maximum impact in your new leadership role* (2012)

- *Lead Your Team in Your First 100 Days* (2013)

- *Your Next Role: how to get ahead and get promoted* (2016)

Author's note

The royalties from this book are being donated to Yuwa, an NGO which works to give girls in rural India a better future through football and education.

I will never forget the moment I first heard about Yuwa's work with girls in rural Indian communities, and the football and educational projects it has been running in the state of Jharkhand for the last eight years. I was at a Storytelling Summit hosted by Microsoft in Seattle in March 2017. Franz Gastler came on stage to introduce the challenges that girls in rural communities face – the threat of child trafficking, domestic violence, sexual abuse and being forced into marriage as child brides. As the mother of two daughters, this is just stomach wrenching. Franz spoke eloquently about the work that Yuwa has done to address these issues – first building a girls' football team that has travelled the world, representing India in international tournaments, and then building a school that is nurturing the girls' rights to learn and helping them to develop the confidence and resilience needed to become authors of their own fate and leaders within their communities. This was clearly an inspirational organisation, tackling deep-seated problems with a grass-roots approach.

It was when Renu and Kusum – two of the young footballers – took to the stage themselves to tell their story, that I knew I had to help. Their clarity of purpose and their determination to challenge the stereotypes and be the change was utterly awe-inspiring. Their courage shone through; these two girls are leading change already and with Yuwa's help, we'll see many more girls like Renu and Kusum able to take their future in their own hands and become the type of leader our world so desperately needs. All royalties from the sale of this book go to supporting Yuwa's work in India, and in purchasing this book, you're not only developing your own leadership capabilities, you're contributing to the development of young leaders who are a world away, but who, like you, are burning to fulfil their leadership potential. You can find more about the work of Yuwa here: http://www.yuwa-india.org/

Who this book is for

If leadership is something you've ever thought about, aspired to, started to do or even been doing for some time, then this book is for you! (And if you like exclamation marks, you'll enjoy it even more!!!)

There is no cookie-cutter template for people who make great leaders. You could just be starting out on your professional journey or you could be an experienced leader looking to step up for one final, legacy-defining challenge at its end. You could be ambitious to lead in a global media corporation or burning to create and build your own tech start-up; you could be about to take your first step up into a retail management role, or feeling a little stuck in your current role and needing an impetus for change. Your experience and focus could sit squarely in business or it could lie beyond, in leading educational, charitable or government teams and organisations.

The advice here isn't specific to any one industry or career type. It's a leadership manifesto and a practical manual designed to help people at all stages in their career and leadership journey. As authors, we're both business leaders, so our focus is primarily on business, but the lessons can equally apply to almost any field, be it medicine or government, the arts or science R&D.

And if you're not quite sure that leadership is for you, or that you're up to the job, then we'd especially encourage you to read on. Because, as we'll discuss, the world needs more leaders and it needs to find them from many more places than it does today. Leadership is not just for the traditional, middle-class, middle-aged, privileged set. The world is changing, the doors are wide open and we want to show how you, yes **you,** can step up, be yourself and be a leader. Many of tomorrow's most promising leaders are not currently putting themselves forward and we hope this book inspires more people to do just that!

Acknowledgements

Leadership is not the exclusive domain of some privileged C-Suite enclave; leadership is everywhere and I've been lucky enough to be surrounded by remarkable role models from the earliest age. Huge thanks are (long over) due to the wisdom of my parents – grossly underestimated by their ingrate daughter as you'd expect! – the generous mentorship of many school teachers, the collegiate support of academic colleagues, the lifelong friendship of Giles and Michael, the inspired vision of my Unruly co-founder and soulmate, Scott, the innovation of Unrulies all around the globe, and regular pep talks from the three astounding children, Sunday, Ezra and Lola Rose (in ascending height order).

I am also indebted to the brilliance of friends and founders within the UK tech ecosystem, the experience and honesty of the business leaders who have so generously given their time to contribute to *Stepping up,* and the empathetic and empowering leadership of my current boss, Rebekah, who guides me and so many others through the complex corridors of a global corporation and makes the journey fun! Not to mention the team who stepped up to get this book on the road. *Stepping up* is certainly the better for the super skills of Niamh O'Keeffe, Eloise Cook, Dan Bernardo, Scott Button, Louise Tullin, Josh Davis, Carl Mesner Lyons and Clemency Carlisle. You truly are the dream team, and without you all stepping up to accommodate for my deficiencies this book would not have made it out the door!

Publisher's acknowledgements

We are grateful to the following for permission to reproduce copyright material:

Quotes

Sir Martin Sorrell/WPP: 17; Keith Weed/Unilever: 55.

Artwork

Dan Bernado/Unruly Group: 11, 19, 30, 31, 51, 57, 78

Introduction

We've written this book because we want more people to consider stepping up to a leadership role. It's a crying shame if talent and potential is squandered. We want more people to step up and be the best they can be. For their own good, for the good of business and for the good of the world. Why is this message so important now? Because today's business world is one that needs more leaders, from a more diverse range of backgrounds. The world is changing, and it's changing faster than at any point in history. We live at a time when technology is driving innovations in how people live, work and communicate with such speed that it can feel almost impossible to keep up with the future as it unfolds around us.

In a changing and unruly world, our leadership culture needs to adapt too. The old assumptions and methods won't hack it in a world where change and the challenges it brings are relentless, volatile and unknowable. The opportunities of today can't be steered by the executive committee, captured in the annual report or addressed by a five-year plan. This book is born from a belief that it's not the CEO in an ivory tower who's going to drive the innovation and decisions that turn potential into progress: it's the everyday leaders, in all shapes and sizes of organisation, at all levels, and with all sorts of different experiences and perspectives.

In other words, people just like you.

What makes a leader? We think the answer to that question is changing, and that the traits of great leadership are evolving as our world becomes faster-moving, more connected and more digital. We've written this book to show what we mean by the new model of leadership: where empathy can be as important as experience, an innovation mindset matters more than IQ, and leaders need to show as much kindness as they do courage. What that means for you as an emerging leader, and how you can develop these key skills, are the central focus of the book.

The good news is, opportunities to step up to a leadership role have never been greater than they are today. Organisations of all sectors and sizes are recognising that the old, hierarchical model of leadership cannot provide all the answers in this new era. A good business needs leaders at all levels, and of all ages. It needs digital leaders, data-literate leaders and leaders who understand the trends and technologies reshaping their industry.

That means there are more ways than ever to step up. And that doesn't have to mean you want to be a CEO or start a fast-growing company. You can lead in all roles and with all levels of experience. How you shape your stepping up journey is something that will be personal to you. We want to help you unlock your potential to lead in a way that is authentic, meaningful and effective for you.

Stepping up could be about taking on your first leadership or management role. It could be about changing your career, or leaving employment to start up on your own. It could be about changing the way you run a team already under your management. Whatever your circumstances, you will face the same issues we all do: of changing attitudes, changing technology and our fast-moving rollercoaster of a world. This book is about equipping you to understand and respond to that change and developing your ability to lead yourself and others through it.

We'll take you on a five-step leadership journey, from understanding the nature of our changing world to establishing a personal leadership mission, developing your leadership toolkit, building a brilliant team around you and empowering it to deliver brilliant results. We'll bust the myths that hold back too many people from fulfilling their leadership potential. We'll take you inside one of the fastest-growing UK tech companies of the last decade, and share some of the secrets of its success. And we'll offer a range of practical advice, tips and exercises that allow you to plot out your own leadership plan, whatever form that may take.

Along the way, we bring in advice from inspirational leaders we've worked alongside, people who are the heart of some of today's most successful and innovative businesses. And we'll be repeatedly asking you to stop and think what all this means for your working life and leadership future.

Sound good? Let's get started.

Your *Stepping up* journey: the five Vs

In the course of this book, we're going to cover a whole load of different ideas, tips and techniques for stepping up to a leadership role. We've organised them into five key stages, from your own personal development as a leader to how you engage and harness the talents of other people to build your team and deliver results. These steps cover the five 'Vs' which we think are essential for any aspiring leader to master:

- **Vision:** understanding fundamental changes in your industry and turning them to your advantage

- **Values:** grounding your leadership in a mission that really matters to you

- **Velocity:** powering up new skills to give your leadership journey momentum

- **Votes:** Finding, building and inspiring a brilliant team to make the dream a reality

- **Victories:** working as a leader to enable and deliver the best results

Step 1 Vision: reset the rules

#TL;DR *In a world that's moving faster than ever before, how do you get to grips with change and turn it to your advantage?*

We view today's age of accelerated change as a reality, a challenge, but primarily an opportunity for emerging leaders. Change is something you can turn to your advantage: a new trend or technology is something you could be one of the first people to really understand, and make work for your business. The first step to becoming a leader is to immerse yourself in what is changing within your chosen industry, and to be one of the people who is shaping the way things will be done tomorrow. You need the vision to see the way of the future, and to be the one who takes advantage of it. This section will cover:

- How the world is changing and why that matters for you on your leadership journey

- How you can turn change to your advantage: tracking and responding to key industry developments

- The opportunities change offers: to become an expert on a new trend, and to experiment with new ideas cheaply and quickly

- Why we need to reset our leadership culture: with new and more diverse leaders

Step 2 Values: make it matter

#TL;DR *Why do you want to lead and how can you make your development as a leader authentic and meaningful to you?*

One of the most important steps to becoming a leader is understanding why you want to lead in the first place. Is it simply for the extrinsic benefits of salary and status, is it to leave your mark, or is it to fulfil a deeper desire to have an impact in a way that matters to you? We believe that the best leaders are those who want to change things for the better, and to tackle some of the big challenges the world faces, from climate change and emergent epidemics to data privacy and social fragmentation. And you don't have to be a big name CEO to contribute to those efforts. In this section, we will look at:

- Why you should explore your personal motivation to lead, and the values that it is based upon

- How you can shape and establish a defining leadership mission that will grow and evolve with you through different roles

- How you can put that mission into practice, finding your CLAN and an ideal place to fulfil that mission

Step 3 Velocity: invest in yourself

#TL;DR *How can you develop the skills, mindset and resilience you will need to generate momentum that powers your leadership development?*

We all have leadership potential, but successful leaders are those who build up specific skills and capabilities that equip them for the many challenges of the role. Being a good leader is not just about doing your own job well, it's about creating the environment for others to succeed and grow as well. To do that, you will need to focus on powering up specific new skills, ones that equip you to step up to the responsibilities of leadership. And you need to invest in your own personal confidence and well-being, to ensure you are equipped for the rigours of leadership. In this third step, we will look at:

- The core leadership intelligences, beyond IQ and EQ

- The characteristics of leaders who step up: what they are and how you can develop them

- Proactive strategies for building and maintaining your confidence

- Why you need to invest time and effort in building a leadership network
- The central importance of personal well-being as a leader

Step 4 Votes: invest in your team

#TL;DR *How do you find, build and nurture the team that will make the difference between you being a lone voice and a great leader?*

No leader has ever succeeded alone. To deliver, you will need to build a team around you, of brilliant employees, peers, supporters and advisers. The most important investments of any leader are in their team, bringing together a brilliant group of people, building their trust and confidence and ultimately winning their vote. This section will look at how you achieve that, including:

- How you find great people and manage the complexities of recruitment
- How you can motivate your team and unlock the full extent of their talent
- Why courage and kindness are key leadership qualities
- How to create a culture that enables a team to grow and evolve

Step 5 Victories: deliver brilliant results!

#TL;DR *What can you do in the everyday management of teams or the projects you lead to deliver – and demonstrate – brilliant results?*

In the end, all the brightest ideas, the best intentions and the boldest plans hinge on one thing: delivery. Whether it's a company vision, team strategy or project plan, it may sound great, but can you actually get it done? If you want to boil down the essence of great leadership to a single attribute, it would be the ability to inspire and deliver results. Creating the magic blend of purpose, people and process that delivers the precious cargo in one piece. Being the enabler that somehow allows everything else to fall into place. This final section will share our experience on how to achieve victories as a leader, with focus areas including:

- Why you need to provide constant clarity as a leader, in planning, communication and people management

- How you can navigate the tide of uncertainty you will face as a leader

step one

VISION: reset the rules

1

Embrace a complex and changing environment

#TL;DR *A fast-moving world means there are more opportunities than ever to envision the future and step up to a leadership role*

All change!

Think of the first time you took a selfie, used a hashtag or read about fake news. It's probably in the last few years, or even the last few months, but it will feel much longer. A decade ago, smartphones and social media were in their infancy; now they are all but ubiquitous. We are living at a moment of profound and rapid change, where new tools and technologies are transforming how people live, work and communicate. Today's overnight sensation can be tomorrow's status quo, and become so faster than ever before.

In response to this change, every industry is being reinvented every single year; and in incremental ways, businesses are reinventing themselves over months and even weeks. Words, ideas and technologies are entering the common consciousness at a dizzying rate. There is an unstoppable torrent of new information and ideas, much more than any one person or management team can keep track of. Yet people still look to leaders for a vision of the future and that's why you, dear leader, need to start thinking about the future of your function/ business/sector, understand how it's developing right now and start to imagine how you'd like it to develop in the future.

What are its current strengths, weaknesses, opportunities and existential threats? What in an ideal world could it become? Having a clear vision of where you want to get to in the future is the best way to harness the potential of so much change and will give you the best shot at building a future business that you want to be a part of.

This presents your first challenge and your first opportunity as an aspiring leader. On the one hand, the pace of change is something you will need to invest time in if you want to make sure you're keeping up: immersing yourself in the new developments that are changing the industry in which you work. Equally, this puts you in an ideal position to develop a vision – or at the very least an opinion – on where your industry is headed, and start playing a leadership role.

When your business is entering unchartered territory, and there isn't a rulebook to follow, you get the chance to write a new one. You can become the expert in something that no one else properly understands. You can provide the new ideas that will give your business competitive advantage. And you can do that just as well as a graduate recruit as you can from the boardroom. In fact, you are often better placed: working on the coalface in a hands-on role, with superior digital knowledge and fewer accumulated assumptions about how things should be done.

The pace of change is great news for emerging leaders. The opportunity to lead, to put forward new solutions and get listened to, is much greater than it used to be. You no longer need to serve your time and patiently climb the corporate ladder to be a leader. Instead, you can win a leadership role through the strength of your ideas, your vision for the future, and your ability to navigate and bring about change.

In this uncertain world, a leader can't just be someone who is a budget wizard, a people management alchemist and a results junkie. You'll need to be those things, and we'll talk about them later in the book. But before all of that, you need to be someone who gets change, who develops a vision of what it means for your industry, and at the same time recognises the uncertainty of a world that's moving faster than ever before. So buckle up!

Words of wisdom: Appreciate shifting patterns

The leaders of the future will have to be able to cope with a continuous fast pace of change. Whether from climate change, digital development, the geo-political environment, the sharing economy or any other new macro developments—the pace of change we experience now is not going to slow down. Leaders will have to quickly appreciate the world's shifting patterns and create/adjust their products and services to match.

> *This generation of young leaders are impressive. They are tenacious. They have to be.*
>
> **BARONESS MARTHA LANE FOX, FOUNDER OF LASTMINUTE.COM, CHANCELLOR OF THE OPEN UNIVERSITY**

Make change work for you

The speed of change in business is opening new doors for you as an aspiring leader. How can you take advantage? You'll need to take a persistently proactive approach, working to identify new opportunities, putting forward new suggestions and experimenting with different approaches. Here are some of our top tips for how you can make change work for you.

GET CURIOUS

The obvious product of change is uncertainty. Businesses are suddenly facing a future that is the equivalent of trying to navigate a cruise ship through heavy fog. You sort of know where you're going, but you can't see the destination and you don't know what might be coming the other way. For an organisation, that can be scary. For you personally, it's a huge opportunity. When companies are crying out for navigators of uncharted waters, it's the perfect moment to step up and become one.

Start by being curious, very curious, about your team, your business and your industry. What are the big hairy problems your company is trying to solve right now? What does your boss need to pole-vault over troubled waters? Find out which white papers are being produced by trade bodies in your sector, carefully read the latest press releases from competitive businesses and see whether you can spot any patterns. Follow a relevant trend from inception to the current day. How has it evolved in the last three months and the last three years? Now think about how this trend might develop in the next three months, twelve months, and the next three years. Repeat the exercise for other trends, always looking for patterns. Repeat this often enough and your brain will be primed to look for patterns in your business, and you'll soon find you've got plenty of opinions on what the future of your business could look like. And not a crystal ball in sight!

TEACH YOURSELF

Identify an area where you can develop specialist knowledge and expertise that allows you to stand out. Choose an area that genuinely excites you! It could be about how you work together as a team, or communicate with customers. It could be related to product innovation or changing legislation that affects your sector. Whatever you choose, invest time and energy in becoming the in-house expert on your chosen topic: set up search alerts for your chosen keywords, subscribe to daily or weekly newsletters from authorities in your chosen field, read everything you can get hold of, attend seminars and events, try to meet established leaders in the field.

Then be generous about your expertise and work to spread it within your company. Share breaking news on your social profiles, offer to host lunchtime lunch 'n' learn or Q&A sessions; share key material and ideas with your bosses, whether that's via a simple email or a strategy white paper. Turn your learnings and ideas into a shared initiative which people can buy into and take forward.

Words of wisdom: Be curious

If I have one piece of advice, it's go after what interests and excites you, even if it seems risky. There's no 'best' path to the C-suite. It's a winding road with many interesting stops along the way, so search out roles that interest you and make the most of them because having a variety of experiences will make you a better leader. Of course, this doesn't mean rushing from one experience to the next. I really think it takes 2–3 years to learn something well, so take that time to learn and squeeze the most out of every job you take. And don't be in a rush to manage people, it's not the only way to be leader.

If you don't know exactly how to get your next role, do informationals with leaders who inspire you, have lunch with people who are working on cool stuff, and ask lots of questions. The most successful people I know are extremely curious. They aren't embarrassed to ask questions and they're always striving to learn more. They also know what they bring to the table. No one knows everything, so be confident in what you know, lean into that, and then be willing to stretch yourself. If you're not being challenged, you're not growing. Hone your skill set and remember that confidence comes with experience. Give yourself the time to earn that experience.

CHRIS CAPOSSELA, CHIEF MARKETING OFFICER, MICROSOFT

BACK YOUR IDEAS

Another by-product of rapid change is that good companies know they need good ideas, and they care more about the strength of new suggestions than the source. In a good company, it doesn't matter if you're new to the business, fresh out of school or not used to making decisions. What matters is having an idea, a solution or a suggestion and having the courage to step forward and share it. It's more likely than ever to be listened to and put into practice.

You should take advantage of this new licence to think and contribute to the important decisions. Familiarise yourself with the key decision-making moments in your company and find out the best way to input your ideas. Try putting forward your suggestion at the company All-Hands meeting, emailing the CEO or asking to be invited to a strategy session. Back your ideas. We know you've got some!

TRY THINGS OUT

Today, you can start a business for £12 in less than 24 hours. You can create broadcast content on your smartphone. You can communicate with almost any public figure via social media, or at least try to. The barriers to pursuing your big idea and making something happen have never been lower. The technology at your disposal means you can do things quicker, more cheaply and more collaboratively than ever before. You have the capacity to experiment, and you need to use it.

Whether you're working for someone else or considering starting out on your own, experiment with a new idea – it could be a new way to advertise, a new platform for communicating with customers or a new productivity #workhack. With communication and distribution channels evolving so quickly, the most efficient way to learn is by doing. Try something that's quick and cheap and see what you learn from it. If you can share your learnings and questions on Twitter or LinkedIn, better still, as you might get some helpful answers, find some like-minded people and at the same time position yourself as an experimenter in the field.

Action: Cast your mind back to when you started your career. What's changed about how you do your job; which new tools are at your disposal; what new opportunities has that created for you?

MAKE A LIST OF THE TOP THREE. WHERE COULD YOU CATCH UP OR GET AHEAD?

Why we need to reset the rules

We need to reset the rules on our leadership culture, making it more diverse, more representative and more open

Change in business today is a reality, which every leader needs to understand; and it's an opportunity for those who turn it to their advantage to power personal leadership growth. We also believe that change is a necessity, and that stepping up isn't just something for you as aspiring leaders, but something that our entire leadership culture needs to achieve.

Why? Quite simply, because business leadership in the UK and US is still very much in the grip of those who are male, white, middle-aged, heterosexual and from privileged social and educational backgrounds. Here are some of the sobering facts: only 7 per cent of FTSE 100 CEOs are female (in fact there are more FTSE 100 chief executives and chairmen named John than there are female CEOs), and only 8 per cent of FTSE 100 directors are non-white.

This is not to say that there aren't brilliant female, non-white and LGBT business leaders, because there are. But there aren't enough; not if we want to reflect the society in which we all live today; if businesses want to meaningfully engage with all their customers; and if we want to build a leadership culture that is broad-based and broad-minded enough to tackle the complex challenges of our digital world.

Why does this matter? Here are a few things to consider:

- Research on stereotypes in advertising compiled by Unilever found that just 2 per cent of ads showed women being intelligent, and just 1 per cent of ads showed women being funny

- A study by Lloyds Banking Group found that fewer than 0.1 per cent of people depicted in UK advertising are disabled; whereas disabled people represent 17.9 per cent of the population as a whole

- Just over a third of non-white Brits were able to name a business role model from their communities, compared to almost three-quarters of white respondents to the same survey

What that shows is there isn't nearly enough representation of different communities and minority groups at the levels where decisions are being made. Which not only risks unfairly excluding and marginalising minority groups, but is fundamentally bad for business, when minorities represent such a growing share of the population and consumer base.

The importance of new leaders stepping up isn't just about us all as individuals, but important for the collective good. You are part of resetting the rules not just for yourself, but for everyone. This is why it matters that new leaders step up, and that they are helped and supported to do so.

If you're from a minority group, then we think the world needs leaders like you more than anyone. And if you are not, think about how your development as a leader can be both inclusive of, and open to, minorities. You will be a better leader if you develop the kind of inclusion intelligence that we discuss in Step 3. This isn't about ticking a CSR (corporate social responsibility) box: it's about reflecting society, the workforce and consumer economy as they are today, in all of their diversity.

The more you can be the change agent, the more valuable you'll become to your business. Why? The research on diversity in business is comprehensive and conclusive; the more diverse the team, the better the decision making. The more diverse the company, the more innovative it is. And the more diverse your workforce, the greater revenues you'll bring in. Improving diversity is a win–win situation for you and your company, so make sure you're a part of it!

Our belief is that anyone with the determination, ambition and will to succeed can become a leader on their own terms. We want to inspire as many people as possible to take on the leadership challenge, discovering what it means to you and the full extent of your potential. And by doing so, we hope to encourage new leaders to step up and remake the image of business leadership in a new and more diverse mould.

Words of wisdom: What it takes to lead

The seven qualities of great leadership, according to one of the world's most successful business leaders, WPP founder and Chief Executive Sir Martin Sorrell

1 **An ambidextrous brain**

    We live in a world increasingly dominated by data, but if all you can do is read a spreadsheet you won't reach the highest level. The intangibles of judgement, creativity, intuition and imagination are essential for great leaders, because they are the things that make innovation happen. They're just as important as logic, financial literacy and an eye for detail. This applies in pretty much any industry, from advertising and marketing services to software development and engineering.

2 **The ability to argue**

    It's annoying when people disagree with you, but an argument is usually a more constructive exchange than a conversation in which everyone wholeheartedly agrees with each other. If a leader is surrounded by yes people they learn nothing. Good people know how to stand their ground and make their case – even (especially) when others don't want to hear what they're saying.

3 **International outlook**

    It's a cliché but sound advice all the same: when people ask me how best to advance their career I tell them to learn Mandarin and how to code (see my next point). Speaking the languages of the great rising powers like China will give you huge competitive advantage in an ever more globalised workplace, but it's not enough by itself. More important than the skill itself is outlook. Top performers are eternally inquisitive, outward-looking and international in perspective. In a world

▶

▶

where ideas cross the globe in seconds, you can't afford to be parochial.

4 **Early adoption**

The same curiosity that leads them to look beyond national borders makes the best people obsessive about the new. High achievers are generally magpies, forever drawn by the glint of new technologies, new thinking and new trends. This doesn't mean they abandon or undervalue the old, but it does mean they are never wholly satisfied with the status quo, they never stop learning and they never stop driving their businesses forward.

5 **Fast decision-making**

I used to say, perhaps unwisely, that a bad decision on Monday is better than a good decision on Friday. With the benefit of hindsight I might have modified that to 'an imperfect decision on Monday is better than the 100 per cent perfect decision on Friday'. Either way, you get the point. Strategy is critical, but without implementation it's nothing. While you strategise and over-intellectualise, others are getting on with things and building a lead.

6 **No butterflies**

This is not a reference to nerves, which afflict us all from time to time, but to those who flit from one job opportunity to another without ever truly committing to an organisation or goal. However bright their wings and however successful they might appear, butterflies rarely make a lasting mark. An old-fashioned view, perhaps – one I inherited from my Dad, who advised me to find something I enjoy, stick to it, build a reputation in that field and then, if I wanted to, strike out by myself. Which is what I did.

7 The will to win

Last but definitely not least, I look for people who really care about winning and losing. I take it personally when we lose a piece of business, or someone leaves the company. After more than 30 years in the job, losing still gets to me! I often plagiarise Bill Shankly, the legendary manager of Liverpool Football Club, who famously said: 'Some people think football is a matter of life and death; I can assure them it is much more serious than that.' That's how I feel about WPP.

ADAPTED FROM A LINKEDIN ARTICLE, PUBLISHED JANUARY 2015

Step 1: Vision—On a page

Takeaways

- Leaders are expected to have a vision of the future, so make a start by working out the key changes in your industry, and how you and your company can get ahead of them
- Make yourself an expert in something that your company, and indeed your industry, does not yet fully understand. Identify a niche you can own and become the go-to person for that in your business. Read everything you can, attend events, and host Q&A and discussion sessions to spread your learnings

▶

- Be confident about putting your ideas forward. Find the best way to do so: at the company Town Hall, by emailing the CEO or asking to attend a strategy session
- Become part of a movement towards more diverse, representative leadership in business: recognise that inclusion and diversity aren't part of the CSR strategy, but about reflecting society as it really is and building a better business as a result

Assignment: Be a DIY expert

Invest time in identifying a key area of change that is relevant to your business: develop your expertise, make proactive suggestions and build a reputation as the go-to person within the company. Key steps:

1 Make a list of three trends, innovations and emerging technologies affecting the industry you work in. Do your research and focus on the one you're most curious about

2 Spend the next month researching it in depth: subscribe to relevant blogs and newsletters, set up keyword Google alerts, join the most relevant LinkedIn group and identify 2–3 events to attend

3 If possible, ask an expert for their view on what this trend might mean for a business like yours

4 Now develop a one-page proposal or two-page white paper with market context and recommendations for how your company could take advantage of the trend. Use the document to start a discussion about how to test your ideas within your team or business

Read and listen

Books

- Kevin Kelly, *The Inevitable: understanding the 12 technological forces that will shape our future*, Viking Press 2016
- Joi Ito and Jeff Howe, *Whiplash: how to survive our faster future*, Grand Central Publishing 2016
- Jane Gleeson-White, *Six Capitals: the revolution capitalism has to have – or can accountants save the planet?*, Allen and Unwin 2015

Music

- David Bowie, *Changes*
- Fleetwood Mac, *Don't Stop (Thinking About Tomorrow)*
- Taylor Swift, *Shake It Off*

Up next

Understanding why you want to lead: what motivates you?

Setting a leadership purpose for yourself: what do you want to achieve?

Finding your CLAN: putting purpose into practice

step two

VALUES: make it matter

Understand why you want to lead

Before you start out on your leadership journey, take some time to understand why you really want to become a leader

Hopefully you're with us so far, and starting to get excited about how you can harness change to supercharge your leadership potential. There's one more step before you can start to begin your leadership journey proper. You need to answer a really important question: why do I want to lead in the first place?

The answer may not be as obvious as it sounds. For while the perks of being a leader are obvious when you think of the earnings, influence and status associated with leadership roles, there are big responsibilities too, to the people around you and the results that you're in charge of delivering. Becoming a leader does mean a big step up, and there's no pretending it will be all plain sailing.

We're not trying to scare you off here! But it's important to be honest and upfront, because while being a leader can be an awesome, phenomenal, richly rewarding experience, there will be times when the stress and responsibility involved can weigh heavy on even the broadest of shoulders.

Leadership can be demanding – on your energy reserves as well as your time – and this is why purpose is so important if you're looking to build a sustainable, long-term leadership career. Working out why you really want to be a leader, and what you want to achieve by doing so, will keep you going when the going gets tough. For some, the extrinsic motivations of status and money are enough. Yet we believe that tapping into your intrinsic motivations – the things that you really care about in life and which drive you – will help you forge a stronger and more lasting leadership mission.

You need to work out what's really at stake for you, before you can start clearing a path towards achieving it. Often that will be a mix of personal and professional motivators. Take a look at the table on page 24 as a starting point.

Which of those factors are most meaningful for you? Are you someone who's about fulfilling professional potential, or unlocking personal value and meaning? It may well be a combination of the two. There's no right or wrong here, but the best answer is the honest one. Before you go any further, take a moment to be honest with yourself about what really matters to you. Those fundamental personal values will provide the motivation you need to fall back on when times get tough.

Personal stake	Professional stake
To make a difference and have a positive impact	To fulfil my leadership potential
To create a better world for my children	To reach the top of my profession
To prove others wrong; to right a wrong or injustice!	To become an industry expert
To make the people I love proud	To build a global reputation
To discover what I'm truly capable of	To leave a professional legacy
To achieve financial freedom	To achieve a top salary

Words of wisdom: The bigger picture

In business, great things take time and great leaders take time to develop. True leadership is when you think beyond yourself. It is about what you contribute to the bigger picture. In the face of major world problems, it is impressive when young leaders are asking how do I make a difference, what is my role in life? This goes straight to the heart of the matter. Purpose cuts through to what real leadership is all about.

GERARD GRECH, CEO, TECH CITY UK

Action: Write yourself a three-sentence answer to the following question: **Why do I want to be a leader?** When you're happy with your response, you can use it to shape your leadership mission. If you want to keep your inner motivations front of mind, you could also stick up your response inside your wardrobe or coat cupboard so you're reminded of why you want to step up as you step out in the morning.

4

Establish a leadership mission

Beyond understanding your personal motivations to lead, you also need to think about leadership mission: the impact you want to have and the difference you want to make

Understanding what motivates you to lead is an important start. You also need to focus on a parallel purpose question: what do I want to achieve as a leader? Beyond my own personal fulfilment, what is the mission that drives me?

If you had the chance to interview a leader like Mark Zuckerberg, Arianna Huffington or Bill Gates about what motivates them, it's unlikely you'd hear too much about money, status and reputation. They're much more likely to talk to you about harnessing the power of technology to change people's lives, whether that's by connecting people with each other, helping them find balance at work or eradicating malaria in the developing world.

Great leaders typically have a mission that's much bigger than themselves; the businesses they build become vehicles for expressing, achieving and amplifying a deeper purpose than profit, one with the potential to achieve widespread impact and leave a lasting legacy.

Of course, having a big, audacious mission that defines our working life is very different from how we were taught to think about careers growing up, when many of us were sent out in the world with advice to choose a career, set off down the 'path' and stick doggedly to that decision, come what may.

If you're lucky enough to have a life-long passion for your chosen career, well that's fantastic (as long as you're actively navigating the changes affecting your sector!), but the reality today is that most of us will have not one career, but many. And we won't follow a linear path, climb a greasy pole or scale a corporate ladder. Instead we'll be finding our way through a maze of different roles, organisations and experiences. A 2016 survey by LinkedIn found that millennials will change jobs an average of four times in their first decade after graduating. Whether we're seeking promotion, better pay or personal development opportunities, we're more likely than ever – and more able than ever – to job hop.

There's nothing wrong with that (though beware of becoming the non-committal butterfly that Sir Martin Sorrell described in the previous chapter) and indeed such gear changes can be highly beneficial. They allow you to experience different working environments and cultures, and often to move more quickly towards your end goal. At the same time, if you are going to have a frequently changing career, you need a leadership purpose to bind it together and give it deeper meaning.

Leadership purpose or mission is something that can flex and adapt to fast-changing circumstances. It will empower you to create or work within businesses that don't know what they will look like in six months, let alone five years' time. It's a compass rather than a map, and one that will help you navigate a world where many of us will end up taking on roles that are being newly created, in circumstances for which there is no case study or rulebook.

Your mission should be what *really* matters to you, a constant that will help you make the big professional choices, build resilience during difficult times at work and keep you focused when the days are long and others around you are flagging.

Your leadership mission could be a problem you want to solve, an idea you want to build, or a partnership with great people you want to pursue. What matters is that it's personal, authentic and important enough to give you the motivation to keep going through tough moments, and a real sense of satisfaction when you clock up the achievements. Purpose is about the impact you want to have in your working life and the legacy you wish to leave behind.

So now you know what it is; how do you go about finding and defining it? Begin by asking yourself some questions. Questions like these, where you envision the future you want, are a great way to limber up your mind as you begin to consider your own, unique leadership purpose:

- What do I believe in and care about?
- What are my passions and interests?
- What makes me happy?

- When do I feel most fulfilled at work, and what do people tell me I'm good at? Is there an intersect between the two?

- Who inspires me?

- What does my ideal day look like? Where am I, what am I doing and who am I with?

The means of achieving your leadership mission might vary hugely, and they will without doubt keep changing throughout your working life, so don't start out by tying your ambitions to a particular company, job title or position. Focus on a broader purpose that can live and evolve with you as your leadership journey unfolds. Remember also that, as a leader, your team will be trying to understand the kind of person that you are. If you're someone who's leading with clear purpose, and that is something which others in your team also believe in, then you stand the best chance of building a motivated and committed team: the fundamental requirement of any leader.

Words of wisdom: Your leadership mission

Empower yourself! Nobody is going to give you permission to quit your job and start a business; or to knock on the door of your chief executive with an idea for how the company you work in could do something better.

Remember this. Many great businesses of our times started from a simple beginning: a good idea that became a clear mission. Today, that opportunity is readily available: the information, advice and digital tools; the network you never knew was in your grasp; the team of like-minded people ready to be hired or energised from within.

MICHAEL HAYMAN, CO-FOUNDER OF SEVEN HILLS AND CO-AUTHOR OF MISSION (2016)

Here are some suggestions for how you can start to work on shaping and defining your leadership mission:

Start with what you know

The first thing is that it's OK to not know what you want! Most of us have been there, and many of us still are. Purpose may be the cornerstone of sustainable leadership, but that's not to say that your mission will come to you in a vision or materialise overnight!

As with so many facets of successful leadership, be prepared to be patient. Having an authentic purpose, clear values, strong culture, defined end goal and an effective strategy for getting there; eventually, you need all those things. But you may have none of them at the outset, just a vague sense that you want to travel in a certain direction. That's fine. Grope, stumble, cast about. You may experience epiphanies. Or not. Things may just gradually become clearer. YouTube started life as a dating site. Twitter as a search engine for podcasts. The swan was an ugly duckling. You can't rush this stuff. Don't be fazed by what you don't know and aren't sure about. Focus on the things you do know and build from there.

Start at the end

At the same time as you're building from the bottom up, drawing on what you know about your capabilities and ambitions, it's also helpful to start at the end. When you've finally donned the pipe and slippers in retirement, what achievements do you want to look back on? What will you tell your grandchildren about what you did? What will you be proud to tell them?

That's hard, because it feels so far away, but it also helps ground you in what you want to achieve, rather than just what you want to do. The means to achieving your end goal will likely keep shifting, but if the end is consistent, you will stand the best chance of getting there. So the end is where you should try and start.

Whatever you do, start somewhere

In the end, however you set your career purpose and in whatever level of detail, the most important thing is that you get started, as quickly as possible. Done is better than perfect, so don't delay in setting yourself challenges and targets to start putting your vision into practice. Don't wait for there to be a perfect moment; there rarely is one, only opportunities you create or seize upon.

Your career purpose is not something to be written on tablets of stone and adhered to as a fixed creed. It's much more likely that it will be, to misquote the immortal words of Captain Jack Sparrow, 'more like a guideline, anyway'. The detail will change and evolve over time; so don't worry about getting it perfect first time.

Action: Three steps towards defining your leadership mission:

1 Make a short, bullet-point list of people you'd like to work with and achievements that would be meaningful for you (limited to three each).

2 Start adding actions and targets to this list where possible, turning the vision into a practical plan you can work to and which gives you a starting point.

---

3 Imagine your 100th birthday (like it or not, an increasing number of us will live to see it!). As you blow out your candles, what personal achievements and impact would you like to be looking back on? And what regrets or 'what ifs . . . ' do you definitely not want to be reflecting on?

FROM CAREER PATH TO LEADERSHIP MISSION: THE NEW MINDSET

FROM: Career path	TO: Leadership mission
Will this look good on my CV?	What will I learn and who will I meet?
What will my next title be?	What new responsibilities should I be looking to take on?
When do I next get a pay rise?	How do I best realise my earnings potential?
Who is getting promoted first?	What new talent should we be bringing in?
How will this further my career?	How will this help me achieve my goals?

5

Find your CLAN

To put your leadership mission into practice, you need to choose your company carefully, love what you do, aim high and network with purpose

Once you have an idea of your leadership purpose, you need to find ways of putting it into practice, and applying it to real-world circumstances. That could be by shifting gear within your current job, and finding new ways to make an impact and develop your leadership skills. Equally, it could mean finding a new job, moving to a different role within your current workplace, or starting up something of your own.

To purpose, you need to add a place and people that can help you make it happen. That may already exist in some form, or you might have to create it yourself from scratch. All of which, of course, is easier said than done. How can you know what you're looking for before you've found it? Well, in many ways you can't, but what you can do is understand some of the criteria you will need to assess different opportunities and routes to goal.

In whatever form it takes, you need to find what we like to call your **CLAN**. It stands for four things:

- **C**hoose your company carefully
- **L**ove what you do
- **A**im high
- **N**etwork with purpose

This is advice that holds whether you're looking for a new start or keen to make the most of your existing career circumstances. Here's what we mean by CLAN:

Choose your company carefully

Whatever you choose to do, you will need the help, trust and belief of other people to make it work. That will include everyone from managers and mentors, to your peer group of colleagues, and a wider network of people you meet online and through events.

The people you work with and alongside are so vital in helping you grow and develop as a person, and ultimately into the leader you want to become. Do they push and inspire you? Are they honest with you about how you could do things better? Are they fun to work with and be around?

I'm often asked for advice by people considering starting their own business. When they ask me what the most important decision is in the early days of a business, I can say with confidence that there's no more important decision than your choice of co-founders (and the same stands for colleagues if you are looking for a job rather than a start-up). Get it right and they'll help you step up and the business scale up; get it wrong and the whole company can come crashing down. My rule of thumb is this: if you're arguing over the name of the company and percentage of company shareholding on Day One, then you've got to wonder what the relationship is going to be like further down the line. Regardless of whether you're looking for co-founders or new colleagues, if you're keen to step up and take on new responsibilities, then working with people who stretch you, challenge you and bring out the best in you will accelerate your development and help you to develop mutually supportive relationships that will underpin your leadership journey.

Of course, 'choose your company' has several meanings here. Sheryl Sandberg famously said that a woman's most significant career choice is her life partner and it's certainly the case that stepping up is a lot easier if you have a supportive partner who champions your corner and backs your ambition with practical support.

The other 'company' you need to be choosing carefully is your place of work. Does it have a good track record of promoting diversity, innovation and professional development? Will there be opportunities to relocate or work across different areas of the business? You need a hospitable environment in which your leadership potential can flourish, so this is the moment to look before you leap!

If you're considering jumping ship from one business to another, before you sign on the dotted line be sure to base your decision on available data ('Best places to work' awards or diversity data for larger corporations), social recommendations (such as Glassdoor), and, wherever possible, face-to-face intelligence from people working within the company now. With LinkedIn, you're a click away from meeting prospective colleagues and understanding what makes them tick and how they feel about the company they work for. Don't be afraid to reach out. Find someone who'd likely be in your team or thereabouts and ask if they'd be happy to meet for breakfast or beers. They'll be pleased to meet you (if they're good prospective colleagues!) and will give you a clearer sense of whether you'd be likely to fit in and flourish in their world.

Love what you do

This may sound like an obvious point, but it bears repeating. Quite simply, you have to be passionate about what you're doing if you want to make a real success of it. The work is too hard, the challenges too numerous and the setbacks too frequent to have it any other way.

You need to be doing something where you could have a bad morning, even a few bad days, and not be discouraged from carrying on. Loving what you do is core to having the motivation to keep going, whatever hurdles you may face.

And that's why having a leadership mission is so important: meaningful success isn't just a series of milestones to be ticked off the professional bucket list; it's a burning desire to succeed at something you actually care about that makes it worthwhile getting out of bed on a cold, dark morning when the last thing you feel like doing is emerging to face the day.

So find a job, create a career or build a way of working that you can pursue with passion and then give it everything you've got. Because you'll need everything you've got (and more than you ever thought you had!) if you want to keep on stepping up.

Aim high (but appreciate what you've got)

Be ambitious in the long term. Don't just think about what your immediate next step is. Jump forward a few moves and consider what the landscape will look like from there. What trends and changes are affecting your work; which competitors both existing and potential should you be thinking about; what does your dream client or customer market look like and how could you get there? Be ambitious for yourself too: where do you ultimately want to end up and what are the stepping stones that will get you there? At the same time, don't expend all your energy looking for the next role. Never forget to do your current job with grace and gusto!

In your current role, don't be satisfied just to do what works, think about what else you could be doing to deliver brilliant things that move you and your business forward. This means developing a mindset where you're never entirely satisfied or settled, and are always looking for a new way to improve, innovate and do even better next time.

That's as true for dealing with immediate business issues as it is for thinking about your own career trajectory. How can you turn a solid client relationship into a great one? A satisfactory product into a market-leading one? A well-honed team into an award-winning one?

As a leader, you have to be living in the 'now' while keeping an eye firmly on the future: the opportunities, innovations and threats that tomorrow will bring. When you're figuring out your next leadership move, don't settle for something you feel entirely comfortable with; go for the ambitious option that will challenge you and take you to a new level. Always be aiming high. And stepping up!

Action: Think about your 'now, near and next'. Pen a two-line answer for these three questions:

- How is the work I do **now** giving me opportunities to develop as a leader?
- What are the **near** opportunities to develop that I could take on?
- What is the **next** step for me in my leadership development? How do I reach it?

Network with purpose

Networking makes many people shudder, but with the right mindset it shouldn't be a chore, a bore or a bogeyman. In fact, we'd argue it's one of the single most important routes to unlocking and accelerating your leadership potential. If you want to be an effective leader, you'll want to be well networked both within your organisation and beyond, across your sector. You don't network because it's fun to collect business cards, you network because you need to meet people to build business context, procure market intelligence, spot patterns, meet potential clients, source the best colleagues, influence decisions, and look around corners to see where the next big ideas are coming from.

Whether you're trying to hire the best talent into your team, looking for a new role, or seeking someone to mentor or advise you, it's generally a good plan to get out there and start networking. If you're someone who finds that a bit intimidating, take it from us: no one is entirely confident going into a room full of people; everyone has social anxiety on some level, and the only thing you can do is be yourself, be interested in other people, and be clear to yourself about what you're hoping to achieve (yes, it's back to our old friend purpose!). Having said that, if you're not too time constrained, then attending events with an open mind and a view to letting serendipity take its course can sometimes yield surprising results. Either way, now that you're stepping up, it's time to conquer your fears and throw yourself into it. If you want more networking hacks flick straight to Step 3 where we really get into the nitty-gritty of how to build a network with purpose.

Sarah says: Taking your next step

Too many people think about their careers as a game of snakes and ladders. You're either up or you're down. It's better to see it more as noughts and crosses: moving pieces sideways, forwards and diagonally to build a winning position; going in different directions at different times depending on the circumstances. Here are a few different moves for you to consider on your own leadership board:

- **Move up:** when did you last get promoted, change role or take on new responsibilities? If you're not feeling challenged in what you already do, it's

---

probably time to start thinking about – and asking about – what else you could be taking on. Don't wait around, hoping to be recognised or tapped on the shoulder; begin a conversation with the people that matter in your organisation. Start with a clear idea of what you want to do and how else you could contribute beyond your current role. Make suggestions about how that could be achieved, with a view to creating a win–win situation that gives you additional responsibility and gives the business additional value, whether that's a straightforward promotion or involves creating a new role or team to grow a new area of the business.

- **Move across:** It might not be the right time to move up and you could benefit from taking a sideways step. This doesn't have to mean treading water. You could be developing skills and experience in a different part of the same business – or on secondment at a sister company or different geography. In an age when collaboration and cross-functional working are prized capabilities, this could be an incredible opportunity to learn new skills, meet new people and gain a more holistic view of the business. A lateral move to broaden your experience and skill set can very quickly provide the launch pad for your next upwards leap.

- **Move diagonally:** left-field moves are often worth considering too. It could be a move into an adjacent industry, a shift from practitioner to academic, becoming a freelance consultant or setting up a business of your own. You'll still need to weigh up whether it's right for you: will you love what you do and does it allow you to aim high? Does it match the leadership mission you're shaping for yourself? Many

▶

leaders reach a point where the only way to pursue that purpose without compromises is to create your own vehicle, a business where you set the mission, culture and values. That's a big step, and shouldn't be taken lightly, but for many people who do, it's the best move they ever make.

Words of wisdom: Climbing the grid

You may be driven to 'get to the top' but sense-check that desire. Ask yourself, 'Why do I want it? What does "the top" look like to me? What does it mean to me?' Do you only want to be the boss because you think you should, because you think that's where the ladder goes? Perhaps you are better as a specialist, an independent contributor.

I like to think about a career as a grid instead of a ladder. You want to balance your functional specialism with leadership hierarchy. Where do you want to be on the grid? Where are you happiest and can offer (and receive) the most value out of the relationship you have with your employment? Have an honest conversation with yourself about what motivates you, what you want in your life. Leadership, like a specialist capability, is a skill and not everyone has it naturally or enjoys doing it.

DEIRDRE MCGLASHAN, CHIEF DIGITAL OFFICER, MEDIACOM

Step 2: Values—On a page

Takeaways

- Understand why it is you want to lead: what combination of extrinsic and intrinsic motivations are making you want to take this step? Start with your personal values and ambitions and go from there.
- Define a career purpose that can follow and grow with you throughout your working life, as you take on different jobs, roles and responsibilities. Purpose should start with something that matters to you and the impact you want to make. It doesn't

matter if you don't have all the answers to start with; work out a direction of travel and the rest will follow.

- Think about finding your CLAN: Choosing your company carefully, Loving what you do, always Aiming high, and Networking with purpose.
- Don't see your leadership journey as a game of snakes and ladders either, where you're always either up or down. Think of it more as a noughts and crosses grid: you might have to make some sideways or diagonal moves to keep progressing and that's absolutely fine.

Assignment

Define and write down your own leadership mission. It should be sufficiently ambitious that you won't be able to achieve it next week or next year but practical enough to be attainable in the next few years. List some immediate steps that you can do to take you in the right direction of travel.

Read and listen

Books

- Michael Hayman and Nick Giles, *Mission: how the best in business break through,* Penguin 2015
- Seth Godin, *Linchpin: are you indispensable? How to drive your career and create a remarkable future,* Piatkus 2010
- Adam Grant, *Originals: how non-conformists change the world,* WH Allen 2017

Music

- Mamas and Papas, *Make Your Own Kind of Music*
- Fleetwood Mac, *Go Your Own Way*
- Puccini, *Nessun Dorma*, from *Turandot*

Up next

The new leadership intelligences: digital, entrepreneurial and inclusive

The principles of *Stepping up* leadership

How a leadership network can take you further, faster

The central importance of building your confidence and safeguarding your well-being

step three

VELOCITY: invest in yourself

This next step is going to explain how you can develop your leadership toolkit by cultivating a range of core skills and intelligences, growing your leadership network and prioritising your own personal health and well-being. In short, this chapter is all about you, for 'you are your own best thing' in the words of Toni Morrison's *Beloved*. We want to make sure that you've got the right kit and can build the momentum required to get your leadership career to take-off velocity.

Before we get down to the detail, there's one thing you need to remember. Every leader you now admire was once someone with no experience, setting out on their own journey, taking risks and trying out things they didn't really know how to do. You might not feel 100 per cent confident, and that's absolutely fine. No one has all the answers, however confident they might look and however competent you might believe them to be. What you already know matters less than your willingness to get stuck in and learn.

A love of learning, and the compulsion to continuously explore new ideas and put them to the test, is one of the hallmarks of a great leader. You can learn from books, blogs, video tutorials and TED talks, you can learn from trying things out, and you'll learn the most when the things you try go wrong. You'll surround yourself with people who are smarter than you, and learn some more from them. And over time you'll develop the confidence, the experience and the track record to do even better.

You will never stop learning how to lead: that is as true for experienced CEOs as it is for emerging leaders starting out. Becoming a leader isn't some linear pathway, where accomplishments and milestones are neatly ticked off. It may look that way from afar, but when you get up close and personal to leaders you admire, you'll often find that their leadership journey has been more of a messy, uneven and difficult scrabble up a cliff face, where they've had to zig and zag and veer and pause for breath and find footholds they can't easily see. And it looks just as steep halfway up as it did at the base of the cliff when you first set off.

So before we get down to the practicalities of which leadership skills you'll want in your toolkit, our simple message is this: be brave, step up and believe in yourself! Don't be the one who rules out possibilities before you've given them a try; and whatever you decide to do, throw yourself into it with everything you've got. Because stepping up can be a leap of faith, there will be moments when you feel as though you're about to lose your balance and take a nasty fall. Remember, we all feel that way sometimes, no matter how much we've achieved and how far we've scaled. And in those moments when you hit your stride, and you're leading an awesome team, doing meaningful work and delivering great results, there's really nothing so enriching and exhilarating. If you're serious about stepping up, it will take you on the ride of your life and, once the endorphins are flowing and you've got a taste for the journey, you won't want it any other way.

When I'm coaching team members to try something new and challenging, I often tell them that they get an 8 out of 10 for having the courage to show up and take part. So give yourself a pat on the back for getting this far. You've committed to being here, you're open to new ideas, so now let's get stuck in.

6

Expand your leadership intelligence

In today's connected world, good leadership is as much about your digital experience, entrepreneurial mindset and inclusion intelligence as it is about your IQ or EQ

The idea of what makes a good leader has changed over time and we've come a long way from the days when a dominant personality and didactic style were the uniform leadership traits of respected chiefs.

Today, most people would agree that there is no single model of good leadership. How could there be, when there are so many different leaders, with their own personalities, motivations and styles of doing business, and so many different types of businesses and organisations to be led? Your own leadership style needs to be something you develop and get comfortable with over time: how do you present yourself and your company in the most positive light; inspire and motivate your team; deal with challenges and setbacks? Over time, if you regularly reflect on where you're strong and where you struggle, and if you continuously solicit and learn from the feedback of those you trust, you'll find a way of doing things that works for you: one that embodies your values and reflects you as a person.

Leadership shouldn't be a mask you put on at work and take off at the end of the day; if that's how you think about leadership, it will place you under enormous psychological stress, run the risk of making you look insincere, and will always end in tears. If you want to step up for the long haul, it's time to be authentic and real. You need to really mean it and that means it has to come from the heart.

That said, there are certain traits that make for good leadership, which you can develop and shape into your own distinctive style. One of these is undoubtedly emotional intelligence (EQ), the ability to manage and harness emotions – the impulses and motivations that shape our behaviour – and to empathise and connect with those of others. EQ is important, but it's not the only extra intelligence you will need to step up to a leadership role.

We're also living in a digital world, where it's necessary to understand how changing technology affects your business; we're living in a fast-changing world, where you need an entrepreneurial mindset to rapidly respond to threats and anticipate opportunities; and we're living in an increasingly diverse society, where business leaders are expected to meet the needs of a much wider range of constituent groups among your workforce and your customers. You need to invest in more than just IQ and EQ. Let's have a look at the different mindsets we think you need.

Digital intelligence (DQ)

All too often digital is seen as a siloed department, a standalone industry or a niche sector within the economy as a whole. The truth is, digital now pervades all aspects of how we live, work and do business. It's estimated that 42 per cent of digital jobs exist in what are thought of as traditionally non-digital industries – such as the public sector and financial services – and according to Tech City UK, the digital economy is growing 50 per cent faster than the rest of the economy, accounting for 1.64 million UK jobs. The growth in digital is unlocking huge opportunities, new ways of thinking and working. But it's also unleashing new threats, particularly around cyber security and data protection. All of which means that every business, on some level, is becoming a digital business. So every leader must now be a digital leader.

That doesn't mean you need to have been coding since you were out of nappies. If you're fluent in programming languages that's a great head start, but if you're not there's no need to despair. You could complete an online course at the Digital Business Academy, or invest in a day course at Decoded, a brilliant digital skills business that helps people understand the building blocks of digital in just a day. If that's not enough, you could learn to code in 12 weeks at immersive developer boot camps such as Makers Academy. If that all sounds too much, then you could start by surrounding yourself with people who do have digital skills, asking them questions and learning from them as they tackle real-life digital challenges.

Digital intelligence isn't about a skill set that involves the nuts and bolts of writing code. It's about a mindset that appreciates the digital impact and ramifications of everything you do as a business. It's a mindset that sees the digital opportunity and asks how digital tools and platforms could help you grow your business, reach new customers, reduce your costs, develop your product or optimise the services that you offer. It's also a mindset that recognises the digital risks. How quickly could a competitive business enter your market and imitate your social marketing strategy? Are you mitigating security risks that technology poses to your business and your customers? And it's a mindset that asks the questions that matter. Should you build or buy that new product feature? Is your digital strategy mobile-first? How do you find and motivate digital natives on your team? How will AI disrupt your business model in the future?

As a leader you don't need to be the one with all the digital expertise, but you do need to invest the time in getting under the hood of the digital platforms most relevant to your business. If you're not prepared to roll up your sleeves and learn to speak digital, your opportunities for stepping up will become increasingly limited.

Action: There's no shortage of places to hone your digital skills. *Primer* is a handy app for bite-sized digital marketing tips, and the Digital Business Academy offers a range of helpful, free online sessions, giving advice on how to start a digital business, build a digital brand and use social media to reach your customers. Search online and through LinkedIn for relevant meet-ups in your area and take advantage of specialist events and training opportunities.

Words of wisdom: Digital intelligence

A learning mind-set is essential for current and future leaders. The world is changing at a pace never seen before. Technology is one of the key factors in this change. It is disrupting traditional business models, hierarchies and roles. Yet how many of us can say that we truly understand the technologies behind the screen, the ones and zeros sending instructions to machines? Less than 1%? It is probably even less than this if we look specifically at leadership. The leaders of tomorrow will embrace technology education with both hands, no matter what age or stage of their career they are at. They will seek to cultivate a deep digital literacy and confidence which will allow them to ask the right questions and truly innovate from understanding how to use code to access APIs to implementing artificial intelligence across their business.

KATHRYN PARSONS, CO-FOUNDER AND CEO, DECODED

Entrepreneurial intelligence (EnQ)

You may be someone who is already running their own business, who aspires to start up on their own, or is more at home in a larger corporation. It doesn't matter either way, because no matter the size of the business you're part of, in this age of constant disruption, you'll need an entrepreneurial mindset to fulfil your leadership potential. Why? Because businesses of all sizes are struggling to respond to sweeping market changes and to effect change at the pace they know is needed to survive and thrive in a time of heightened uncertainty – whether that's the product of digital transformation, workflow automation, or legacy business models that are no longer sustainable.

There are many different kinds of entrepreneurs, but entrepreneurship is essentially about the ability to break down barriers, the courage to break through processes and the confidence to back yourself and your team as you break new ground; to deliver on your promises and do great work without getting trapped in the weeds of process, bureaucracy and 'can't do'. Entrepreneurs are doers, who get the best out of themselves and other people. The good ones inspire focus, commitment and incredible performance.

There are many entrepreneurial qualities that will stand you in good stead if you're stepping up your leadership game – having the grit to go from nothing and keep on building in the face of intense competition or its more insidious twin, market apathy; having the bravery to test the riskiest assumptions first and fail quickly if you're wrong; having the agility to constantly course correct, revise your assumptions and then adapt the role you play within the business.

Developing an entrepreneurial intelligence is about identifying a real problem that needs solving and then working out the simplest, leanest and fastest routes to solving that problem and delighting your customers. It's about behaving like the owner of a business, caring passionately about what you do, and bringing on board brilliant people who can make things happen, mitigate your weaknesses and help turn your vision into a reality. You may not be planning to become an entrepreneur,

---

Action: Try looking with fresh eyes at a problem you're currently facing or a major piece of work you're doing. How could you simplify the issue or the process? What's the riskiest assumption that you need to test first? And which colleagues/clients/academics/peers/competitors could help you get there faster?

but you do need to learn to think and behave like one if you're serious about stepping up your leadership potential.

Inclusion intelligence (InQ)

Next time you're in a meeting, try something. Keep track of how much speaking time men are taking versus women. Count how many times women are interrupted while speaking. Count how many times men do that interrupting. You'll almost certainly find that it is men who do much of the talking, and almost all of the interrupting.

As many studies have shown, the sad reality is that too many women in business hold themselves back from saying what they think: because they either fear that they won't be listened to, or they're worried they'll be thought of negatively because of what they say.

That is a major issue in its own right, but also the tip of a much bigger iceberg: namely, the very poor levels of diversity and inclusion in many businesses today. As we've already discussed, despite some progress towards shifting the dial, most businesses – especially big ones – are still led by a very narrow stratum of our society. Lack of inclusion is a problem that stretches across a whole range of groups. It's about ethnic and economic background; gender diversity; people who are denied equal representation because they are disabled, have a medical condition or because of their sexuality or political views.

Until all those voices, perspectives and experiences are being heard, business will not be able to do a good enough job of representing and meeting the needs of every customer. Which means, today's leaders need to be as inclusive as they are digital, entrepreneurial and emotionally attuned. They need not just to encourage, but to actively champion a wide diversity of voices that contribute to key decisions. Inclusion isn't part of the CSR strategy; it should be a fundamental part of your leadership ethos. It's not about doing good, it's simply good business.

Action: At your next team or management meeting, make a point of running it a different way. Invite in people who would not usually attend, give those who would not normally speak a defined role to play, and encourage those who would typically speak to listen and learn.

Words of wisdom: Invest in yourself and be yourself

Investing in your own leadership development is vital. You can't devolve responsibility for your own path. The only person who can explore your potential is you. The opportunity for you to develop may be spotted by others, but you have to do the work to bring it out. Be in charge of

▶

your own path. I always found it very helpful to learn from other leaders, ask their opinion, and attend sessions where I could listen and learn from their experience. Leadership development is an iterative process – something you have to do every day. You may slip back and will need to remind yourself. Get yourself good mentors and ask for alternative points of view.

HELEN MCRAE, UK CEO, MINDSHARE

7

Develop your leadership toolkit

The stepping up leader will be mission-obsessed, put their people first, never wait to be asked and be their team's optimist-in-chief

Building on the new leadership intelligences, we now want you to think about what these characteristics mean in practice. What does being a digital, inclusive and entrepreneurial leader look like in the everyday context of managing projects and teams? How can you apply these intelligences in either taking your first step up to a leadership position, or changing the way that you run things in your existing role? What will your step up look like?

To help you work that out, we have identified four core principles that we believe are central to stepping up and developing and fulfilling your potential as a leader.

1 Be mission-obsessed

Stepping up is about making your mission – personal and collective – absolutely central to everything you do as a leader. After all, there's no point having a guiding purpose if you don't stick to it. Everything you do should be in some way contributing to both your personal leadership mission and the mission of the business you run. Use mission as a benchmark for the decisions you make and the actions you prioritise. The purpose you set for yourself and your team should be the lens through which you view which clients to take on, which products to build and

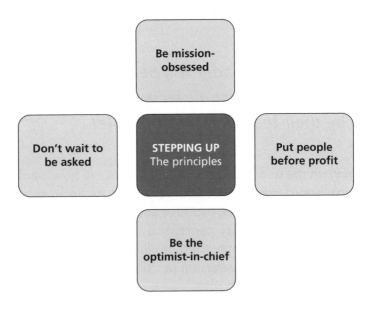

how you work together as a team. Keep asking yourself, 'Does this feed into the mission? Does this help take us closer to where we want to be?' And if the answers are no, you probably need to start reconsidering.

2 Don't wait to be asked

Stepping up to become a leader means you can't afford to be someone who hangs back and waits to be asked. Whether it's taking on a new responsibility, shaping your next career move or trying to change the way your business works in some way, you need to take control of your own destiny and take responsibility for making things happen. While not everyone is a naturally assertive character, it's important to recognise that the days when talent simply rose to the top are gone. You can't expect that your good work will be recognised and rewarded purely on its own merits; you have to make your good work visible, be your own champion, ask to take on new responsibilities and make suggestions for things to change. And if you're already in a leadership role, then there is even more reason to get on with making things happen. This is a world where you have to shape your own future: be brave and dare to grab the opportunity with both hands!

3 Put people before profit

Stepping up means recognising that you have to consider the needs of your people alongside those of the bottom line. While many might argue that the single most important responsibility of a leader is to grow and protect profit margins or 'shareholder value', this approach ignores the fundamental reality that there are no profits without people, and there is no business of any scale without an engaged, committed and motivated team to sustain it. We're not saying you should go out and spend like crazy or always pay top dollar for your team; on the contrary, for most self-motivated people, having meaningful work and autonomy over how they spend their time are more important than lavish perks and more money. What we are saying is, make your primary leadership focus the building of a best-in-class team, with processes and priorities that make them feel like the best-supported, best-recognised and most-empowered team in the business. Get that right and the team will pay for itself many times over.

4 Be the optimist-in-chief

Stepping up is something that requires a giant dose of optimism and positive energy, whether you're taking on your first leadership role or seeking to take your current team to the next level. Positivity is infectious and we enjoy being around people who have a positive take on life. When leading a team, you want to be the figurehead who is setting the collective sights high and also the activist who is spreading confidence and belief that you're going to get there. A negative mindset can hold back a whole team, and a pessimistic tone from the top – even in a very subtle way – can be destructive to company morale and can quickly undermine your business goals. Always search for the silver lining in any situation and think of your role as COO: Chief Optimism Officer. Trust us, the realities of everyday leadership will provide all the corrective realism you need!

Action: Start putting the stepping up principles into practice. Take the four challenges below, give yourself a week and record your progress. How did you do?

```
              ┌─────────────────┐
              │  One way to bring│
              │   my leadership  │
              │  mission to life │
              └─────────────────┘
┌──────────────┐ ┌─────────────┐ ┌──────────────┐
│  One new     │ │ STEPPING UP │ │One thing I can do│
│responsibility I│ │Principles into│ │to empower my │
│ can take on  │ │  practice   │ │    team      │
└──────────────┘ └─────────────┘ └──────────────┘
              ┌─────────────────┐
              │  One new way to  │
              │  celebrate the   │
              │ achievements of  │
              │    my team       │
              └─────────────────┘
```

8

Build your confidence

As you develop your leadership skills, take a proactive approach to building your confidence: train it and build it like a muscle.

The stepping-up leadership principles we've just outlined all demand a tonne of energy. That doesn't mean leadership has to be about bouncing around the office like a Duracell bunny, high-fiving everyone in sight. But persistent optimism, a focus on mission, the championing of people, and resilience in the face of challenges can tax your energy reserves, which means that you will need to be at your most confident to step up to a leadership role.

Time and again over our own business journeys we have seen emerging leaders failing to take the next leap because of a confidence gap. Not an ability gap, a skills gap or a capability gap, but a confidence gap. The good news is, we can fix this! We can fix it because confidence isn't an innate ability or fixed personality trait; it's a behavioural trait that can be learned, developed and honed with practice. Think of your confidence not as a fragile vase that you are continually carrying across a marble floor, but as a muscle that you will train and build up over time through effort and experience.

Sarah says: Believe in yourself

Today, with my co-founders and exec team I lead a thriving, global business of over 300 people. Yet rewind to 2006, and there was no product, no platform, no clients and only the three of us co-founders. Believe me, I was a long way off seeing myself as a business leader.

At that point, I had no significant experience of scaling a company. The short time I'd spent during university vacations running a greasy spoon café in London and a chocolate shop in the Lake District might have been some preparation for the hard graft of being a small business owner, but it was far from formal training! And for the previous few years I'd been an academic at UCL and then the University of Sussex, where my expertise wasn't advertising technology but American literature.

When we started to get Unruly off the ground, I found myself compiling reports on digital ad campaigns for people who had worked in the industry for decades, when I had never even shot an ad or planned a media campaign before. This was somewhat unnerving but I soon realised that being the person who knows the least means that you have most to learn; and that means you have the most to gain.

▶

> So while you might not have the experience, you can more than make up for it by having the ambition and the appetite to learn and develop. Don't spend time and effort worrying about what you don't know and can't do. Instead, back your strengths and focus on what you can learn. Have the confidence to take on things you might think are a little beyond you; only by stretching yourself to the limits of your abilities will you find out what you are really capable of.

Investing in yourself as a leader will be a constant process over the course of your career. While a lot of the advice in this book is designed for immediate implementation, you'll never stop having to build your confidence as a leader. And that's especially true if all your great work is being recognised and you're being rewarded with new opportunities to step up! Here are some proactive strategies to help you build your confidence muscle.

Be kind to yourself and smile

There will be moments when things get tough, when your knees are knocking and your throat constricts. At points like these don't be tough on yourself, be kind to yourself. Ahead of big events, rather than agonising over speaking notes, I (Sarah) find it more helpful to talk to myself in the mirror and say out loud to my reflection the words my mum would say if she were in the room with me: 'You're going to be just fine. You'll do your best and that's all that matters.' Boy, is my mum wise! Honestly, management MBAs are overrated when you have the wisdom and experience of people around you to help you on your way. (And a tip to everyone who's caught up in their own career progression – make the time to call your mum or other family and friends who supported you through those formative childhood years; they are part of the reason you are where you are today and they will appreciate a heartfelt THANK YOU when they're least expecting it!).

In fact, I rarely walk away from any mirror without smiling at myself (or chuckling at my funny ways!). Whether I'm washing my hands, walking on the treadmill, or opening up my wardrobe in the morning, I make a point of this ritual because smiling releases serotonin, which slows heart rate, reduces blood pressure and just makes me feel . . . happier about myself, kinder to myself.

I've heard my seven-year-old daughter, Sunday, when she's about to try something new and scary, say to herself in a fierce little voice, 'You've got this, Sunday' and I've started doing the same thing. It's simple, you can start today, and when repeated frequently it helps to build long-term confidence and resilience. If you're serious about stepping up, you're going to face lots of challenges, so it's good to be kind to yourself, and develop inner voices that support and reinforce you rather than voices that criticise and complain.

Learn from mistakes and move on

What to do when you've had a go at something, it's not gone to plan and your confidence takes a knock? Remember the words of James Joyce: 'Mistakes are the portals of discovery'. You might not get the outcome you want every time, but it's when things go wrong that you have the most to learn. Your worst day at work is actually providing you with your best opportunity to learn. The war wounds you pick up on the journey all help to make you a successful leader and equip you to do things differently and better the next time.

This is what we mean when we talk about resilience. It's about learning to take the knocks in your stride and using those knocks to your advantage. A big mountain takes a few goes to climb, and it's what you learn on early attempts that allow you to conquer it eventually. Whatever you do, don't stew over your mistakes – beating yourself up about a poor presentation or botched project launch will not help you up your game. It's a waste of energy because the past is out of your control so focus on the future instead – on what you can change so you will feel more satisfied with your output next time round. Accept when you've got something wrong, identify the learnings and move on.

Words of wisdom: Develop a thicker skin

Outstanding leaders are confident, motivated and never stop learning. I was fortunate to have very strong female role models; my grandmother and mother. What I look for in my leaders are the 3 Gs:

- *Grind: by which I mean the willingness to keep at it, business is not easy and you have to be prepared to keep on moving forward;*

- *Grace: not everything goes right and I seek out people who possess grace under pressure;*

- *Grit: I need people who are laser-focused about achieving their goals.*

My consistent advice to the emerging generation of leaders is to develop a thicker skin. Not everyone is going to like you or agree with you, and you can't be too sensitive.

DEBBIE WOSSKOW, CEO, LOVE HOME SWAP

Words of wisdom: Try on different styles

If you choose to lead, read books on leadership but also observe others and see what works for them. Take the time to notice and learn how people lead. Don't be afraid to try on different styles until you find the bits that suit you, that feel right and natural for you. Just like you'd try on clothes before deciding which to buy – what looks good on the hanger might not suit you when it's on. But when you're comfortable, you are confident. And there's nothing more powerful or magnetic than confidence.

DEIRDRE MCGLASHAN, CHIEF DIGITAL OFFICER, MEDIACOM

Self-monitor and seek consistency

As a leader, you need to be constantly observing and monitoring yourself, your behaviour and decisions. In what kinds of situations do you display great talent? In what kinds of situations do you perform suboptimally? Watch what you do when you're under pressure. Observe how others react to you day to day; do you notice when someone is trying just to please you rather than give you bad news? Do you know how to be humble and accept the very worst of yourself whilst striving to do better next time? The more emotionally intelligent you are, the more you are able to regulate your own impulses and emotions and behave with consistency. It is described in Buddhist circles as the ability to tame your monkey mind, i.e. rather than being at the mercy of your mind chatter and mood swings, you can grow the capacity to choose how you respond emotionally to events and how you regulate your own emotions in a productive manner. Some people meditate or use mindfulness techniques to help them to improve how they manage their own emotions.

Monitoring and mastering your emotions is key to leadership progression because nobody wants to work with an emotionally volatile colleague or work for an unpredictable boss, who's scowling one moment and high fiving the next. That's confusing, unsettling and very unlikely to bring out the best in your team if they don't know where they stand with you or what to expect from you one day to the next. It's not just how you talk to people in person that matters, it's how you talk on email too – a notoriously difficult medium to master! It's easy to be misunderstood on email and to unintentionally come across as curt, dismissive or rude, so be mindful of your email tone, keep it positive and if in doubt, skip the email altogether and suggest you talk to each other in person.

Words of wisdom: Monitor your state of mind

Are you aware of your state of mind and how it is influencing you when making decisions? Would you make a more optimal decision if you were in a better state of mind? Perhaps you would listen better, you would not miss the opportunity right in front of you if were thinking calmly and clearly. I try to empower my team to be in the right state of mind to make the right decisions. I also teach them to appreciate that everyone's reality is unique and they need to check for understanding to see if everyone heard the same message.

JAMES LAYFIELD, SERIAL ENTREPRENEUR AND FOUNDER OF CENTRAL WORKING

Seek regular feedback and say thank you

At the same time, you can't be the only one who is monitoring your performance. Relying solely on your own instincts to self-assess is the equivalent of taking your temperature with a thermometer that's been run under a hot tap. You need an accurate measure, and one of the best ways to build confidence is to regularly seek feedback from those you work with. Your own individual perspective on your work and impact is by its very nature subjective, narrow and partial. You might be worrying too much about something that isn't even perceived by others as a problem, or you may be unaware of a blind spot in the way you work.

Either way, there are lots of real-time opportunities for you to seek feedback from peers and managers. Do simple things like asking colleagues how they thought a client meeting went, and if there's anything you could have improved upon so you know to include it next time. More formally, you could ask your HR team to run a 360-degree feedback exercise on you that allows all levels of your team to give feedback, up, down and across the business. Whatever you're most comfortable with and however you choose to gather feedback, make sure that you're proactively seeking it out and cross-checking your own instincts against what others are seeing and saying. When you receive negative feedback, whether or not you agree, be sure to listen attentively and openly, say 'thank you' and mean it! Feedback is a precious gift on your stepping-up journey, a power-up every bit as valuable as the golden mushrooms that give you a speed boost as you race around the track in Mario Kart.

Keep practising!

You don't need to be perfect to be an awesome leader, but you do need to keep practising what you do and remain self-aware about your blind spots and the ways you can improve. Back in the 1960s it famously took four Liverpool lads 10,000 hours of band practice to become The Beatles and your commitment to self-improvement is critical if you're going to truly fulfil your leadership potential. Practising what you do is a proven way to improve self-confidence, especially at key milestone moments when you have that big interview or client presentation that you really want to nail. Put in the time to prepare; that way you'll feel more in control and know that you've put in the effort and done your best regardless of the outcome.

Words of wisdom: Focus on your strengths

You can't simply tell someone to be confident. People don't hear, they see. Your behaviours and actions will speak louder than any words. To build confidence, we used Gallup's StrengthsFinder to focus on strengths, rather than weaknesses. For the under-confident people, especially women, we found it unhelpful to talk about what you are not good at – instead we celebrated and encouraged self-awareness on a person's strengths and unique talents.

We also organised skills development 'mega-events' annually for the company, whereby people were pushed out of their comfort zone – for example, having to write/produce/star in a theatrical play – and this showed the younger people how the senior management were not good at everything (!) and showed the senior folks that the young people had unknown talents tucked away. A good lesson for all!

EDWINA DUNN, PIONEER OF TESCO CLUBCARD, CEO OF STARCOUNT AND AUTHOR OF *THE FEMALE LEAD*

Appreciate your achievements

For over-achievers, it can be difficult to take the time to reflect on what has already been achieved. We urge you to take a moment at the end of every day to consider and recognise what you have achieved in your life, and in your day. With this longer perspective, you may notice that you're the only one from your university class who has set up their own business, or properly appreciate that you financed your move to a new city without any help from your parents, or so on. There will be accomplishments that are unique to you and your situation. Appreciate them. Be mindful of the good stuff in your life, and how you got it. To achieve a deep-seated core confidence, you will need to appreciate yourself and what you have overcome to be in the position you are in today. Confidence is not all about tomorrow and what can be achieved in the future, it is also about the past and what has made you the person you are today. Give yourself credit for how far you've already come.

Be grateful

People who approach life with a sense of gratitude appreciate the chances they have been given, and are more open to future opportunities. When things don't go as planned, people who have learned gratitude are more resilient and faster to bounce back because they can put setbacks in perspective. When opportunities come their way, they feel luckier about having the chance to do more, to achieve more – and this kind of openness leads to a positive spiral of success and confidence. Customers reciprocate loyalty when they feel that you truly appreciate their business. Employees and team members reciprocate support and hard work when they feel that you truly appreciate their hard work and efforts. Think about small ways to show your gratitude to the people that matter to you: whether it's a simple email or thank-you card, or a personal gift.

Be generous

A confident leader is a generous leader. Rather than thinking of leadership as a zero-sum game ('You win, I lose'), the confident leader will play a non-zero-sum game ('We can all win. Just because you win doesn't mean that I lose'). Confidence implies that there is room for everyone, that we are all in this together and that there are plenty of gains for everyone! A confident leader is happy to collaborate with peers, seek out mutual wins, and pay it forward, supporting and cheerleading the next generation of leaders. What does generosity look like in practice for a leader? It is about giving credit and recognition, giving great assignments and opportunities to your people, giving your time, sharing contacts, giving your support, and anticipating how to help others.

Go from to-do to ta-dah!

Rather than a constant focus on what's next on the to-do list, how about making a list of what you have done – 'ta-dah!' This can be an inventory of achieved tasks that remind you about how productive you were today, this week or since you got the job. Delivered my project on time – ta-dah! Spoke up about my concerns at the meeting – ta-dah! Helped the finance team to solve their sales force queries – ta-dah! Try it, and see how many items you can put on your ta-dah list. It's fun, not least because you probably haven't used the word ta-dah since you were a kid doing forward rolls and trying to stand on your head – good metaphors for business today! If there are not enough ticks on your ta-dah list, then all the more reason to try harder the next day.

After a while, you train yourself to focus on outcomes not actions, and on increasing your sense of satisfaction at jobs well done. A focus on what you have achieved will make you realise that you are making a difference and will help to build your confidence. Turn negative thoughts into positive ones to reduce anxiety and increase your own belief in what might be possible. For example, instead of thinking 'maybe it won't happen', say to yourself 'it might happen'. These subtle shifts in attitude and thought pattern create more optimistic and buoyant energy which may impact a more positive outcome. Focus on your achievements as well as objectives yet to be realised.

Remember the journey is the reward

When you achieve a significant goal, you won't be the same person you were when you set out on the journey. The process of achieving your goal and the experience you gain along the way will have changed you. This is why the journey is the reward. The discipline of working hard to achieve your goals will have given you strengths, skills and experience that equip you to do more and go further. You may have learned resilience, patience, courage. You go to a higher level of experience, which means that what was challenging before is now seen in a different light – placed in a better perspective, no longer as daunting as it once seemed. After all, you did it once, and you can do it again. You can rise to the next challenge. And so it goes on: confidence builds confidence. One success leads to another because underpinning each success is a story and a journey that strengthens you. At any one time we are in the middle of a longer journey; take comfort from this and realise that arriving at your destination is not the only marker of success. It's what you are doing now, along the way, that builds you into a leader. So don't just focus on the end goal: appreciate the skills and experience you are building now and every day.

Words of wisdom: Banish negativity

Life is more complicated now and not smooth-sailing. However you want to step up, whether that is going for a promotion, or starting a new business, if it is what you want then I urge you to go for it. I have never regretted taking professional gambles. The risks pay off. Step up on your own terms and don't try to mimic anyone else. Build on your own strengths. Put any negativity to the side.

Of course you need to continue to learn and get feedback but be yourself and forge your own path. Work hard and be nice to people. Err on the side of generosity. Be a good person. Try to do a good job. Some people still think that success just happens. I don't think that is the real world. For example, it is very difficult to build a company and is much harder than the pictures painted. The rewards are personally and professionally very satisfying, but it is also hard work.

BARONESS MARTHA LANE FOX, FOUNDER OF LASTMINUTE.COM, CHANCELLOR OF THE OPEN UNIVERSITY

Action: A simple daily practice will help build up your confidence. You might have heard of random acts of kindness (also very cool!). Well, along the same lines, try performing a random act of courage every day and you'll become practised in recognising what scares you, and grow in confidence through pushing yourself out of your comfort zone and realising that you can achieve more than expected.

9

Cultivate a leadership network

Behind every successful leader is a network of supporters and confidantes; one of the most important investments you can make in yourself is to cultivate that leadership network

Networking can be a bit of a dreaded word for some people, conjuring up the image of warm glasses of wine, random conversations and people looking over your shoulder for someone better to talk to.

But make no mistake, building a network is one of your biggest power ups as a leader. It's a vital investment; just as important as developing management skills. In today's fast-moving market, you will likely hold different leadership positions in different companies at different times. You can't (always!) take your great people with you. But your network does come with you: it grows with you, extending and evolving as your leadership journey progresses. If it's built on strong foundations of purpose, generosity and reciprocity, your network will play a key role in providing opportunities that you could have never dreamed of.

Why does a good network matter so much?

IT'S HOW YOU LEARN

A great leadership network will include many different types of people and organisations. But fundamentally, a network should be full of people you can learn from, whether that's the next generation of up-and-coming innovators, your industry peer group, or subject experts in your field.

Sometimes a difficult problem you face as a leader is better discussed with someone who has no stake in the outcome of the decision. Not everything can be dealt with in-house and it's good to have a network of formal and informal advisers and friends who can act as sounding boards. Having a network will help you learn from the other interesting players in your sector, who will often be the best people with whom to share ideas and learn about what's coming down the pipe.

IT'S HOW YOU MEET PEOPLE WHO CAN HELP YOU SUCCEED

Your business will need many other people to be successful, whether they're working in it as an employee, working with it as a partner, client or supplier, investing in it as an angel or venture capitalist, or commenting on it as a journalist or market analyst.

And while there are formal channels for meeting all these different people, the relationships you build will be much stronger if they're developed in more informal, less transactional conditions. Someone you meet over breakfast at an event, or through speaking at a conference, gets to know you when you're not in the middle of doing business. That provides a much stronger basis for a non-transactional, trust-based working relationship than if you only ever meet people while 'at work'.

IT'S HOW YOU GET KNOWN

When you're building a business, building its profile is a critical success factor. A large part of that success will be driven by how you as a leader tell the story of your business to key constituencies, from potential recruits to investors, clients and the media. As a leader, much of your most valuable work will take place outside the office walls, engaging with people who can help your business, and whom you can help and offer opportunities to in turn.

The same applies if you're building a leadership career within someone else's business. At this stage, the story you're building is your own: you might be looking for a new role, or people who could help and advise you on taking the next step. Whatever stage you're at, it's never too soon to get yourself out there: you never know when the connections you make and the relationships you build may turn out to be needed. Building a network is a virtuous circle too, and generates momentum over time, as current contacts are comfortable introducing you to their contacts, and a warm introduction is far more likely to yield results than a cold call from someone you've never heard of. A case in point is this book – we get leadership coaches approaching the business every week, but Niamh and I were introduced to each other by Matt Stevenson, the brilliant, inspirational CEO of footballing charity, Street League. Matt and I go back a long way and if he makes an introduction I know it's in my best interests to follow up. The rest, as they say, is history!

Reciprocity is the key to successful networking so find ways to start building relevant and reciprocal relationships with the people you'd like to be part of your network. Think about the tools you have at your disposal that could bring value to your network, and at the same time consider which of your contacts will bring most value to your business, then find the sweet spot. Could you interview them for your company blog, host an event and ask them to speak on a panel, or invite them to be a thought leader on a podcast you produce? There may be a valuable introduction you can make or a prospective client you can bring to them. Try hard to make networking worthwhile for everyone involved – for you and for your contact, for their business and for your business; that way you can build lasting relationships rather than having a ten-minute conversation or an unfocused 'catch up over coffee'. And if there's a golden rule of networking? Be sure to give more than you take.

Action: Map your existing network. List:

- Three people you know within your current business who could help you step up
- Three people you know outside your current business who could do the same
- Three companies or organisations that could help you step up if you knew them better

Against each name, identify what you could do in practice to help them achieve their goals. If you're looking for inspiration on what these goals might be, check out their social profiles for recent updates or look

---

at the company's recent press releases – that's what they're keen to promote right now. You've got your conversation starter/email opener right there – now what are you waiting for?

Words of wisdom: Building a network

My advice to the younger generation is to think bigger than your desk. Understand the priorities of your boss. Listen to the message from your leaders. I find it is still rare for people to really listen – and even more rare to act on what they hear! Listen and think about how to personally contribute to the business. Build a powerful personal brand. Use social platforms to build your leadership brand. You can use your online presence to be clear about what you believe in and what is important to you. Define what you care about. This will send positive signals to your customers and your teams.

PAUL FRAMPTON, CEO & UK COUNTRY MANAGER, HAVAS MEDIA GROUP

A leadership network: who's in it?

In many ways, your network is an organic creation that will grow around the people you meet at events, socially and through introductions; you never know quite who's going to be at a given conference or who you might unexpectedly encounter in the bar. That is all part of the power of getting yourself out there, and the fun of it too!

At the same time, it's worth putting time and effort into shaping your network and seeking to include at least some of the following types of people:

MENTORS

Many leaders enjoy talking to people a few steps further on the journey, who have been through – and survived! – similar experiences to their own everyday problems and big hairy challenges. If you're looking for a mentor, it's good to seek out people who have held roles similar to your own, who can empathise with your situation and are prepared to listen, encourage and help you navigate key challenges. There's a vogue for mentors and mentoring initiatives as we write in 2017 and the expectations are sometimes unrealistic. A mentor will not tell you who to fire or how to land your next big client. But they can listen to your challenges, ask probing questions and suggest some ways forward that you may not have considered. So find out about mentoring initiatives within your business or sector and always pay it forward – if you're lucky enough to have a mentor, think about who you could be mentoring in turn. It's never too soon to start helping others step up, and in our experience the most valuable mentors are often just a year or two ahead, which makes their insight timely and the advice bang up to date.

If you thought that all mentors are traditional 'grey-beards', you'd be wrong. If you're someone who can't immediately tell your Snap from your Insta, consider a reverse-mentor: a younger adviser who's plugged into new media and emerging platforms that you'd like to better understand.

PEERS

Just as you'll benefit from people who have previously walked in your shoes, you need others who are living the same challenges as you right now. A peer group is one of the most important parts of any leadership network, and from our personal experience it is the most effective group for helping to hone your leadership skills.

People often look surprised when they hear I've never had a mentor, but that's because I've been incredibly lucky to have inspirational co-founders to learn from along the way. While mentors can be a good sounding board, it is your direct peers, those living through the same challenges and everyday realities, from whom you will often learn the most. They have their fingers on the pulse of what is happening right now and can point you to emerging trends and time-saving hacks. Think of it as part idea sharing, part relationship building and part therapy!

Don't wait to be invited to a peer group meet-up; if there's nothing that meets your needs, then take the initiative and start your own. Your peer group should extend beyond those you work alongside, so make the first move to build relationships with your opposite numbers in companies you admire.

TRUTH TELLERS

One of the biggest risks for any leader is that you become surrounded by a coterie of people who tell you only what you want to hear. This isn't just a problem for CEOs in 25th floor boardrooms either: it could be supportive colleagues who are trying to be helpful but not giving you the straight-shooting advice you need to get better. You need a truth teller: someone who is going to give dispassionate, constructively critical and very direct input on the issues you're grappling with. Whether that's a business coach you pay or a trusted client you ask to be your 'critical friend', having a dose of straight talking fresh from the outside world is an invigorating corrective to your assumptions and can often bring a refreshing change of tone and perspective.

THOUGHT LEADERS

Building a network shouldn't just be about doing a better job today; it should also help you to be better informed about what's going on in your industry and what's coming round the corner tomorrow. Get to know the people who are at the cutting edge of the newest trends, technologies and developments in your field. Cultivate the researchers, academics and experts who are shaping the future of your industry. They may not help solve the problems you face today, but they could well give you competitive advantage tomorrow. Do you have any unique data or research that you could share with them to confirm their latest hypothesis or add to their upcoming industry presentation? If you can help them out and be associated with their research, the halo effect will be powerful and positive for your personal brand.

CHAMPIONS

Whatever stage you're up to on your leadership journey, you'll need people who are on your side and championing your cause. No one becomes a successful leader alone, and most people who run major businesses have had a succession of people who believed in them, invested time and advice in them and whose recommendation and support was key to their progress. A champion is someone who will actively further your cause. If you're lucky enough to have a champion in your organisation, don't forget to keep them up to date on your latest projects and achievements – give them the material they need to sing your praises when you're not around, and don't forget to see whether there's anything you could be doing to help them with their goals. Even champions appreciate a helping hand!

SOCIAL BUDDIES

Most people's conception of networking revolves around IRL (in real life) events, but you should also be looking to social networks too. You're probably already using tools like LinkedIn and Twitter, but are you making the most of them? Do you actively engage with people you want to get to know, post your own content and opinion, and join relevant LinkedIn groups? An increasing amount of networking now happens online and the power of digital is that it allows you to reach people who are outside your immediate sector and geography. Grab the opportunity to build a contact base of people online who can offer you a whole new perspective on the opportunities to step up in your industry and beyond.

Action: Make a network wish-list:

- Someone you would like to be mentored by
- Three internal and three external peers you could get to know better
- A potential truth teller and thought leader
- Someone who could help advance and champion you as a leader
- Three people you would like to get to know, and could engage with through social media

---

A leadership network: how do you build it?

We've explained why a leadership network is important; now here are some tips on how to build yours:

MAKE IT RELEVANT

I only ever go to events where I feel I can learn something. Talking to somebody is a bonus. And it's a lot easier to talk to someone when you've just heard a kickass lecture or watched a synapse-tingling demo. I ask myself three questions when considering whether to go to a networking gig:

1 What can I learn from this event?
2 What value can I bring to this event?
3 How can I ensure it brings value back to my business?

The first question determines which events I choose to attend: I only go to places where I'm confident there'll be new experiences, ideas or viewpoints I haven't come across before. On adding value, I focus on tweeting, speaking and asking questions, and then being alive to the other people in the room: saying hello to the person who's attending alone and looking shy, introducing people to each other, even showing people the way to the loos. Don't attend an event if you're not willing to throw yourself into it, and to make yourself useful!

On the third point, you can get off to a good start by reading up on participants in advance, identifying any clients and connecting with them on LinkedIn ahead of the event. During any presentations, see if you can make notes and share them straight back into the business – turn them into a blog post if you're somewhere really cool. My advice here is don't delay on getting any of this done: do as much as possible in real time, take photos, tweet and write notes during speaker sessions. I don't use business cards any more – too slow and easy to lose – and instead I open up an email on my phone, pop in the email address of the person I've just met and write them a 'hello from Unruly Sarah' email there and then, looping in any relevant people from Unruly, to make sure that the people who will actually get stuff done are looped in straight away! So pick your events carefully, make sure it's relevant for you and your business, then throw yourself into it.

BE ACTIVE AND RECIPROCAL

A network is both an organic creation and a living thing, which will wither and die if you don't nurture it. Find reasons to stay in touch with the people who matter to you, even when there's no immediate reason for doing so. It could be as simple as an invitation to meet, an introduction to someone who may be useful to them, or a quick note to share some nugget of information you think they may find interesting.

By the same token, you need to build reciprocal relationships where you are thinking as much about what you can do for the other person as they can do for you. People who are only ever contacted in time of need will soon recoil from a relationship that feels one-sided and expedient. Be proactive about how you can help and support people in your network; don't allow relationships to drift into a state where it's all take and no give. One way of helping is to be the host – whether that's suggesting drinks in the pub to mark a business milestone or convening an 'innovation summit' themed around a current hot topic in your sector. For sure it's more work, but you'll get so much more out of a group you have yourself convened than being a spectator at somebody else's event.

10

Look after yourself

However big your workload, as a leader you need to be at your best and that means proactively investing in your well-being and knowing when to stop

In an uncertain and constantly changing business landscape, you need to be continually on your toes, making quick decisions and often pulling long hours. As a leader, the stakes are high and every day you'll be challenging yourself and stepping out of your comfort zone.

That makes it all the more important that you put a premium on well-being, both your own and that of your team. In a high-pressure environment, you need everyone to be at their best, and you're no use to your team if you're too tired to think straight or too stressed to sensibly prioritise your workload. The last thing we want to see is your carefully considered and strategic step up followed six months later by spectacular burn-out, so it's worth you thinking about how you can find the magic balance between stretch and stress; commitment and overloading yourself.

Leading requires high energy levels, clarity of mind, and above all an optimism and confidence that transmits itself to everyone around you. You need energy and equilibrium, and that's something that needs to be constantly replenished. So take a look at your diary and start to envision the simple tweaks to your routine that will create the opportunity within a busy 24 hours to get a good night's sleep, at least one healthy meal, enough exercise to leave you out of breath, and some time to think and reflect.

Sarah says: Simple habits can improve well-being

For me, the 30-minute walk to work every morning creates the headspace I need to start the day with a clear focus. It also doubles as my exercise fix. And I sleep like a baby at night. This isn't rocket science, it's about forming positive habits that I know are good for my mental and physical health in the long term. Lavender pillow spray on, mobile phone off. Plump the pillow up, pull the blinds down. These are the bedtime rituals that help get me to sleep. I always shoot for eight hours of sleep, often I only get seven, and occasionally I dip to six, but I love making up for it with long lie-ins at the weekend!

At the same time as looking after your own well-being, you need to closely safeguard that of your people. Part of this ▶

► is about team perks and practices, from having water and healthy food on offer to designated areas for relaxation and opportunities to exercise the body and mind, whether that's gym membership, football leagues, lunchtime jogging clubs, film nights, pilates sessions, or a ping-pong table in the basement. (Unruly's latest addition to our HQ is an augmented reality bouldering wall, made interactive and gamified by our climbing-crazy software engineers.) Be on the lookout for people who may be developing working habits that could lead to burn-out and do everything you can to encourage a culture where long hours are not the norm and worked only when absolutely necessary.

Leading by example is the most effective way to role model this behaviour – I won't send emails after 9pm unless I'm responding to a member of the team – and it's the norm for Mums and Dads at Unruly to flex their working hours in order to make the school drop-off, nativity play, sports day, parents' evening, concert – those life milestones that no parent wants to miss. Find the balance between ambition and well-being, understanding that the two do not need to be in competition if you're in the right company – some businesses will care a lot about your well-being and others less so.

The good news is that the macho/masochistic leader, bragging about late nights and lack of sleep, has become a corporate relic. That's just not helpful and not effective in a time of heightened complexity and constant change, where we need to have our wits about us to respond quickly and problem-solve creatively on the fly.

So as you take control of your stepping up journey, make some well-being resolutions and develop proactive strategies for managing your well-being. From experience, it's more realistic to build exercise or meditation into your current routine wherever possible, so they don't add additional pressures to your diary; and to help you stick to your well-being resolutions, you might find it helpful to enlist the support of your housemates, partner, parents, children, boss or colleagues to keep you honest.

Within the workplace, seemingly small things can have a seismic impact on performance and productivity: for example, the more you can foster a happy and positive culture, the calmer you'll be and the longer you'll live – yes, you did hear that right! Studies have shown that happiness in the workplace is a significant contributor to longevity, so there really is no excuse for letting your workplace well-being slide!

Words of wisdom: Look after yourself

There's a long overdue awakening in Western society taking place that recognises the importance of looking after our minds. The stigma around mental health is starting to fade and many people now realise that mental fitness is just as important as physical fitness when it comes to our health and well-being.

Nowhere is this more important than at work, the place where we spend most of our waking hours. The great leaders of tomorrow understand that the psychological well-being of their employees is vital to ensure their team are not just productive and engaged but also resilient, empathetic, happy and healthy.

Meditation is a very valuable skill that helps develop many of the skills needed to thrive in the 21st-century workplace. Hundreds of research papers a year are now published showing a positive link between meditation and attention,

▶

focus, creativity, memory, immune system, compassion, sleep and more.

Mindfulness meditation is a practice that many forward-thinking companies are now teaching alongside other important wellness initiatives such as nutrition, yoga, sleep and physical exercise.

MICHAEL ACTON SMITH, CO-CEO AND CO-FOUNDER, CALM.COM

Words of wisdom: Secrets to leadership success

Eighty per cent of success is showing up

I'm a huge fan of these words from Woody Allen, one of the most famous directors of all time. It seems simple to suggest that if you are not involved you have no chance of affecting anything, or succeeding, or achieving, but this adage has really stuck with me throughout my career.

It's making the effort to be present physically and mentally, to be contributing, and to be making things happen. Although you shouldn't stop at 80 per cent (the final 20 per cent is what defines you), you would be surprised how many people don't do the 80 per cent – the showing up and getting involved. And once your foot is in the door, make sure you commandeer a coat hook and get a set of keys cut.

If you're not failing, you're not trying hard enough

At school and at home as a child you are always being encouraged to get things right. Getting things wrong is a failure. But in a fast-changing digital world this kind of thinking can result in being too safe and not seeking disruption. We need greater appetite for risk and that can only come with the acceptance that things will fail.

Nobody gets everything right first time, nor should they. We learn from our mistakes and, at the risk of falling into cliché, learn more from them than our successes.

Fuelling change and innovation has never been a smooth process. There are constant hurdles to overcome, but they add excitement. I know from speaking to people involved with the Unilever Foundry that the process is challenging yet extremely rewarding. The more experience you have of what hasn't worked, the more your future work will be better for it.

The difference between ordinary and extraordinary is one little word: 'extra'

About ten years ago now I watched Bear Grylls take to the stage at a leadership conference I had organised when I was leading our global Laundry and Homecare business. He was the youngest British person to ever climb Everest, and was there to talk about the experience of his climb. This was long before his TV show fame. He said something that has stuck with me to this day – that the difference between ordinary and extraordinary is just one little word . . . extra. He puts in extra and that differentiates him from others. And he achieves more.

During a trip to India last year, I was asked to speak to a group of students from the country's top institutions about my leadership methods. I felt this quote rang so true in a nation of 1.25 billion people; one that is second only to China at the top of the population charts. I looked at the classroom and saw a room full of potential future

▶

leaders, but what would set them apart from their peers in their futures? What is it that turns a footballer from top-class professional into Cristiano Ronaldo, a great children's writer into JK Rowling, an experienced politician into a Prime Minister or President? What is it turns the ordinary into the extraordinary? The answer is that one little word . . .

Have fun! Miserable people deliver miserable results

This is one of my own quotes! There are some people who enter a room and suck out all the oxygen, and with that all the possibilities and opportunities go too. There are others who bring energy and confidence to experiment. People who get people to be at their best more of the time. People who bring inspiration, belief, energy and of course some fun! I know which ones I would rather be around – what about you?

KEITH WEED, CHIEF MARKETING AND COMMUNICATIONS OFFICER, UNILEVER

Step 3: Velocity – on a page

Takeaways

- Invest in yourself: your skills, confidence, network and well-being. Don't expect this to happen by magic. Take the time to actively develop and work on these areas, and momentum will soon build.
- As a stepping-up leader, it is no longer enough to rely on IQ and emotional intelligence. You also need

to be digitally, entrepreneurially and inclusively intelligent.

- To step up, you need to be mission-obsessed, putting purpose at the heart of everything you do; you will need to put your people first, become your team's optimist-in-chief, and you can never wait to be asked to take on new responsibilities.

- Be proactive in building your confidence as a leader, treating it not like a vase that could be shattered, but as a muscle that can be trained and developed. Make sure to challenge yourself without setting expectations unreasonably high, and try to learn from your mistakes rather than dwelling on them. Seek regular feedback from the people you work with and be your own supportive inner voice.

- Invest in nurturing a leadership network, of people who can be your mentors, champions and truth tellers. Carefully choose the events you attend and ask yourself what value you can bring. With every relationship you foster, always be thinking first about what you can do for the other person.

- Above all, remember to look after yourself and know when the time has come to stop and take a break. Implement routines that create time to think, and focus on topping up your energies for the challenges ahead.

Assignment

Use the stepping-up leadership principles to do a self-assessment exercise on yourself as a leader. Where are you strong and where do you need to improve? What do you feel comfortable with and where do you need to build up confidence?

▶

▶

Read and listen

Books

- Sheryl Sandberg, *Lean In: women, work and the will to lead,* WH Allen 2017
- Arianna Huffington, *Thrive: the third metric to redefining success and creating a happier life,* WH Allen 2014
- Michael Acton Smith, *Calm: calm the mind, change the world,* Penguin 2015

Music

- Nina Simone, *Feeling Good*
- Pharrell, *Happy*
- Snap, *I Got the Power*

Up next

Why a great team must be your No. 1 leadership goal

How to take a hands-on role in recruiting the best people

Strategies for supporting, nurturing and empowering your people

Why you must be a courageous, kind and above all an empathetic leader

The importance of team and company culture

step four

VOTES: invest in your team

You are not alone. That is one of the most important – and liberating – things you need to recognise as you embark on your leadership journey. Unless you're starting a business as a team of one, you'll be working with other people, and they are your secret weapon in the stepping up journey.

In our fast-paced digital world, the days of the lone wolf leader and visionary CEO, predicting the future and performing business miracles, are now gone. There's far too much going on, too many new developments, technologies and competitors to try and lead the way alone. There are more interconnections and interdependencies than ever before: with customers, suppliers and the wider world.

This is a reality you need to embrace if you want to step up as a leader. So far we've talked a lot about things you can do within yourself to develop a leadership mindset and leadership skills. We've looked at defining a leadership mission that steers the decisions about what you want to achieve as a leader and the impact you want to make; choosing or creating a CLAN, an organisation that will challenge and inspire you; developing multiple forms of intelligence, practising the stepping-up principles, cultivating your leadership toolkit and developing strategies for confidence building and personal well-being. Phew, you've got a lot on your plate! In the words of Dr Seuss, it's a good job you're so footsy!

The good news is this: it's not all about you. As the oft-cited African proverb reminds us: 'If you want to go fast, go alone; if you want to go far, go together'.

Why? Because your team is the single most important aspect of your leadership journey and legacy. More important than the speeches you give. More important than the recognition you receive. More important, even, than the new business you bring in (because without a great team, who is going to deliver it, wow the client and help you bring in more next time?).

The first, best and most important investment you will make as a leader is in your team. Talk to any successful entrepreneur and almost all will readily credit the team that made it happen. Because, while you as a founder might have had the spark of an idea, there are severe limits on how far you take it alone. Without a great team to make things happen, challenge your thinking and spot the hidden icebergs, your big idea will soon find itself stranded on the rocks. It's the same if you aspire to leadership within someone else's company: you might be the one reporting on results to your board or investors, but it's what gets you to that point that really matters, which is the work of the team behind you. Whatever your circumstances as a leader, you will come to rely and depend on your team. And that's exactly the way it should be.

We live in a competitive, highly networked world where it's highly unlikely you're the only business in your field. In that context, your team brings competitive advantage. The company that wins in the long term will be the one with the best organised, motivated and clearly aligned team. An empowered team that's given real responsibility, trusted to make decisions and relied upon to deliver, will achieve great things and save you from many errors and missteps along the way. In a constantly competitive talent market, you need to lead like a politician running for election: continually seeking to win the vote and endorsement of your people.

It's because other people will be so important to your leadership success that winning votes demands a chapter in its own right and this is often the biggest step-change that aspiring leaders have to make. We have tips for building and nurturing great teams; advice for developing the leadership skills you'll need to get your team firing on all cylinders; and concrete suggestions for shaping a culture that will define the identity of your team.

And it starts with the people you'll be working with every day. The people you will be relying on to turn the big ideas into big progress, and inspire and challenge you as a leader at every turn. How do you find and pick the right people; how do you get the best out of them; and how do you turn a group of individuals into a team that is greater than the sum of its parts?

11

Find great people

To hire great people, make sure you're hands-on in the process, identify your dream team, work with them in real time and test for team spirit

It all starts with finding the right people and if you've stepped up your networking, then you'll be in a strong position when a new role opens up with a bunch of people to call up right away. If you really want to get ahead of the game, we suggest you maintain a 'virtual bench' of people you'd like to work with, tucked away in a Google doc on your drive. This should be a list of the people you've met or worked with who have most impressed you with their talent, drive, results or collaborative work-style, be they clients, suppliers or former colleagues. Keep a list of the people you'd like to play alongside in your professional dream team and contact them when a relevant opportunity arises. Even if you're not the hiring manager, referring brilliant candidates is a great way to contribute to your company and raise your profile by becoming a talent spotter.

Once recruitment gets underway, if you are the hiring manager then get as involved as possible in the hiring process – this is not something to be passed off to HR. Your team is too important a matter to be hands-off about; as a leader, you need to be setting the tone for the kind of people you want on your team, and that means getting hands-on in the difficult business of making decisions about who does and doesn't make the grade.

Whether you are running a small team or a big one, you need to be a key part of the recruitment process. And you need to be clear about what you are assessing people against. At Unruly, even though we're now a global team of over 300 staff, one of the three founders is involved in the recruitment process of each and every hire. Why? Because even in a team of some scale, every person who comes through the door has a disproportionate ability to make either a positive or a negative impact. As a leader, you're in the position to enable the former and fiercely guard against the latter.

Wherever possible, stress test the candidate's ability – get them working on a real-life task and see how they perform under pressure. Give them a problem, a whiteboard and a marker pen and watch them solve the problem in real time so you can see their skills in action. Get them working with other members of your team as well and see how they work within a group environment. You can't afford solo artists or prima donnas if you're trying to build a genuine team, with people who will go out of their way to help, support and improve each other. However tempting it might be to hire a star striker on their own merits and nothing else, you should always test for collaboration – businesses have become so complex that collaboration is often the only way to understand and solve the most pressing issues. Even brilliant people need to be able to partner up.

As for what good looks like, well that varies from role to role and from company to company, but it's a good idea to be super clear on the guiding principles and cultural behaviours that your team, department or company is looking for. At Unruly, we're looking for what we call PANDAS (you were wondering what the illustrations were about, right?). By that, we mean people who demonstrate the following behaviours:

Positive and passionate When the going gets tough, Unrulies get going. We come to the table with suggestions and solutions rather than problems and complaints.

Agile Communication, Simplicity, Feedback, Courage, Respect. These principles from 'Extreme Programming' methodology infuse our whole business, from product planning to publisher relations, from site design to business strategy.

No ego and nurturing There's no I in team and there's no I in PANDA. There's a reason for that.

Determined to deliver We believe anything is possible and we'll do what it takes to get there. We agree with Thomas Edison that genius is 1 per cent inspiration and 99 per cent perspiration. Bring on the sweat bands.

Action-oriented A+ players We deliver nothing less than A+ results for our clients; we expect nothing less of ourselves. We keep our promises and measure ourselves and each other by performance.

Social DNA and sense of humour We're hard-wired to seek out competitor intel, swap product ideas, disseminate industry news and share the love with clients, publishers and our fellow Unrulies. But we'll always find time for a bad joke or a funny video.

During the recruitment process, we actively interview and mine for PANDA qualities, digging beyond the standard interview patter to see whether people have what it takes to join our team; and also to make a judgement call on whether they'd actually enjoy it if they got the role. Not everybody wants to be part of a business where everyone is passionate about their work and holds their colleagues accountable for delivering results. You should only ever hire people who you are certain have a good chance of succeeding in the role and enjoying the role within your company. It can be especially hard for some people to move from corporate behemoths to more fluid start-up cultures and vice versa. If there's doubt in your mind, take heed. Hire in haste and you'll repent at leisure. If you're serious about stepping up your role, make every new hire count.

Words of wisdom: Find great people and lose the ego

Hire for strengths not weaknesses

Everyone has weaknesses so it's easy to find excuses not to hire people. Focus on the strengths. What are the two or three capabilities that someone needs to have to really succeed in this role? Has this candidate got them? If so, hire, regardless of weaknesses. If not, take a pass, regardless of other great qualities they might have. (Though it's also OK to hire awesome people sometimes and figure out a role for them later!)

Hire slowly. Fire fast

Your bad hires are usually the most expensive mistakes you ever make. Your best hires, your biggest contribution. So take your time. Easy to say and hard to do, so enforce it through process. At Unruly, our second interview lasts between three and five hours: it acts like a truth drug and leaves people nowhere to hide. Conversely, if someone's not working out, act fast. I've never, ever seen someone fired too soon or too fast.

Lose the ego

Lao Tzu said it best in the Tao Te Ching: *'When the Master governs, the people are hardly aware that he exists. Next best is a leader who is loved. Next, one who is feared. The worst is one who is despised. If you don't trust people, you make them untrustworthy. The Master doesn't talk, he acts. When his work is done, the people say, "Amazing: we did it, all by ourselves!"'*

SCOTT BUTTON, CO-FOUNDER AND CHIEF STRATEGY OFFICER, UNRULY

12

Motivate your team

One of the most important jobs as a leader is to motivate the people on your team: you need to be constantly communicating, trusting and investing in your people, and empowering them to achieve great things

As a leader, one of the most important jobs you have is to motivate, encourage and support your team. No team ever stands still: there will always be new joiners and frequent changes in people's roles and personal circumstances.

Your job is to somehow bind together this merry, ever-changing band; to feed a collective culture and team ethic at the same time as encouraging individuals and helping them to develop their own careers.

It's a fine balance: you have a part to play, but while you may make some key decisions, much of what happens within a large team will be determined without you ever seeing and hearing about it. US General Stanley McChrystal has the right idea when he describes the role of the leader as a gardener: you can plant the seeds, nurture the soil and water the plants as they grow, but only so much is in your control. The growth of people and teams is also organic and uncertain and it's your role to create hospitable conditions that allow your team to thrive. Here are a few ideas to get you started.

Talk to the team

Communication is both one of the most important and often most neglected aspects of good leadership. You might be making decisions and setting things in motion, but are you letting those who need to know – and those who want to know – aware both of what is happening and why it's happening? What we have found is that it is almost impossible to over-communicate; however much you're communicating, some people will still feel as though they don't know what's going on. People don't like being surprised, they don't like being the last to know and they don't like feeling they're in the dark. As a leader, it's always good to talk.

Tip: At team meetings, give your people a dedicated platform to contribute their own ideas and thinking. Always give them an opportunity to ask questions and offer to respond to questions by email too – not everyone feels comfortable asking questions in front of the group.

Trust the team

If you can't delegate, you're dead. A leader who is reluctant to let responsibility pass to their team clogs up the system and makes people wonder why they are not being trusted. It doesn't come naturally to everyone, but unless you show your team that you believe they can and will deliver, you will always be knocking their confidence and restricting their potential to grow.

> **Tip:** Make a rule that you only attend a meeting if you're convinced you'll add unique value to the conversation. If there is no specific reason for you in particular to attend, then don't; it gives responsibility to others who will thrive on it, and frees you up to tackle the rest of your workload.

Invest in the team

Often, you'll be asking a lot of your team and you want them to be prepared to go the extra mile. It's important to reward them financially of course, but this is little more than hygiene: the minimum requirement. It's much more meaningful to reward people with responsibility, recognition and to give them the opportunities to learn and step up themselves. Consider what personal development opportunities your team will benefit most from, and invest what you can in providing them, from training courses through work shadowing and secondments. In addition to formal training, encourage your people to attend and speak at conferences and industry events, so they have the opportunity to build their profile in the broader industry. Make it your mission to help your people develop and grow: your team will deliver even stronger results and your people will get more out of their working life, helping to create a virtuous circle of commitment and loyalty.

Champion the team

Don't forget to find and make opportunities to celebrate the great work of your team; to champion excellence and reward high performance. That not only gives individuals a sense of achievement and satisfaction: it encourages a culture of aspiring to the best level of performance within your business. As a leader, you should take every opportunity to spotlight brilliant work, and to make your team feel good about what they achieve together.

> **Tip:** You don't need grand gestures to make people feel good; persistent and public recognition can be far more effective and have a longer-term effect. Look for small but meaningful ways to recognise people's contribution and achievements.

Empower the team

Give team members autonomy to do their best work – because autonomy is one of the most valued gifts you can give your people, creating a sense of ownership and accountability, and the more ownership your team feel, the better the results they'll deliver. Always be looking for opportunities to help people on your team progress in their careers. Outside of standard promotions, find ways of giving people the responsibility to take on more of a leadership role. Create a fast track where those who want to advance quickly are empowered to do just that. It's a win–win if you have more people, with more experience, moving more quickly into leadership positions; they will feel great about what they've achieved and you'll be gaining a reputation for being a talented gardener, nurturing talent and growing the company's next generation of leaders.

****

Ultimately, your people are your greatest asset, and one of your most important responsibilities as a leader is to support and develop them on their journey. Many leaders find that one of the things they're proudest of is the team they've built and the individuals who go on to enjoy varied and successful careers. Investing in great people isn't just beneficial for the short-term prospects of your business; it's also a long-term bet on what they might achieve long after they've moved on to other things. The individuals you help, who go on to become brilliant leaders in their own right or create their own successful companies, often become the most powerful – and loyal – advocates in your network.

Words of wisdom: The team will help you scale

As a single person, you can build something amazing. But if you want that something amazing to be accessed at scale, you'll need a team around you. Don't be blinded by the celebrity of the leadership personality. Not only are people like Mark Zuckerberg the exception not the rule in terms of his level of success so young and so fast, he did not do it all alone, he has a strong team around him and has provided the company with strong leadership.

DEIRDRE MCGLASHAN, CHIEF DIGITAL OFFICER, MEDIACOM

13

Be courageous and kind

To build a great team you need both the courage to be wrong and the kindness to inspire your team.

Feed 'characteristics of a leader' into Google and it quickly becomes clear just how many different ideas there are about what constitutes good leadership. Early results will include articles promising '7 important traits', '10 impressive characteristics', even '22 qualities that make a great leader'.

There's nothing wrong with that. Good leaders do indeed show many different skills, qualities and aptitudes. At this stage, however, we want to try and boil it down to two characteristics that we think encapsulate great leadership in today's world, particularly when it comes to building and nurturing teams. These are the two, equal-but-opposite qualities that great team leaders will use to encourage, inspire and challenge their teams, and to win the vote of their people time and again.

Courage

The first is courage, which might seem an obvious quality to be associated with leadership. After all, it can take a great deal of personal courage to step up into a leadership role, and move from being responsible only for your own actions and results to those of many other people.

However, we want to suggest that courage is no longer about a macho view of leadership: the hunter-gatherer, alpha fe/male who sets the tone by being the biggest and bravest beast in the jungle. We would encourage you to think about courage not just in its traditional sense, but in some new – and more vulnerable – ways.

The bravery of a leader is the ability to make difficult decisions and live by them; to face up to big or combative audiences to defend those decisions; and to truly be the one with whom the buck finally stops.

Yet in the context of building your team, you will also need to show many other types of courage, and that will require different forms of bravery: the bravery to be yourself, with all your flaws, and to admit that you don't always have all the answers; to face up to your mistakes, and to have the humility to ask your team what you could have done better; and to put your trust in other people and to do one of the things that many leaders find most difficult: delegate.

Here are five forms of courage we think leaders today need to show and role model to their teams.

THE COURAGE TO **BE YOURSELF**

As a leader, you will most likely be spending more time with your core team over the course of a given week than you spend with your close family. What that means is you can't try to be anyone other than yourself. So the last thing you want to do is wear a mask and pretend to be someone you're not. As Steve Jobs said, 'Your time is limited, so don't waste it living someone else's life.'

Not only would that be exhausting, it's also counter-productive. People can see through fakery and if they feel you're being fake that will erode the trust you need to build with the people around you. Authenticity is what people respond to; they want to know about you – what you care about, what motivates you, what kind of person you are to work for. So you don't have an option to be anyone other than yourself, and nor should you want to be.

This book wants to help you be the best version of yourself, but don't get bogged down by ideas of how a 'great leader' is supposed to look or behave. The advice in this book is here to be interpreted and adapted to your own personal style and circumstances. Take what's helpful to you, leave what's not, and be brave enough to always be yourself.

Words of wisdom: Be yourself

Leadership is about being you. It is about understanding who you are and from there, you define your own leadership style. It should be real, natural and not a costume you put on at work. Leadership is not about closing yourself off. Recognise all the best bits and the problematic parts – and from there shape and draft the portrait of who you are. With me, what you see is who I am. I am not afraid to say what I think or to admit when I don't know the answer. Followers want to see the real you – your passions, your curiosity, your real self.

HELEN MCRAE, CEO, MINDSHARE

THE COURAGE TO **TRUST**

Many leaders, entrepreneurs especially, will say that their biggest problem is a reluctance to delegate. It's understandable; when as a leader you are responsible for results and performance, your instinctive reaction is to try and do as much as possible yourself, so you have maximum control over the outcome. Except that control is an illusion, because all you're really doing is creating a bottleneck, depriving your team of opportunities to lead, and adding unnecessary weight to your already heavy burden. Put another way, control creates a dependency culture and suppresses the initiative of other people. Being routinely in the weeds denies people the chance to flower.

Ever done a 'trust fall' exercise before? We bet the first few times, you stopped yourself rather than letting yourself fall freely to be caught by the person behind you. That's essentially how most leaders start when it comes to trusting their team. You know, in principle, that there's someone waiting to catch you, but you aren't quite ready to put that to the test. Getting past that trust barrier is one of the most important things you will achieve as a leader. Until you're prepared to actually trust your team – not just to do things under close supervision, but to make their own decisions, take ownership of their work and take responsibility for their self-improvement – you will never get the best out of yourself or other people. Conversely, when you do put your trust in people and empower them to have confidence in their abilities, the results can be amazing.

THE COURAGE TO **ASK**

For some leaders, the last thing they would ever want is to lose face in front of their team. But if you want to fulfil your potential and keep on stepping up through your career, you need to be entirely willing to look foolish. Ask the questions no one else is asking, especially ones that may seem silly or obvious. If you don't, probably no one will. One of the great fallacies of groupthink is 'someone must have thought of that'. People often keep quiet because they don't want to risk being ridiculed for asking the obvious question. And that can be how important things are missed, bad decisions get signed off and mistakes get made. It's your responsibility to ensure everyone knows it's OK to ask.

As a leader, you can set the tone that says nothing is off the table, no idea is too weird or wonderful to be considered, and no question too obvious or silly to be discussed. That may sound like a small thing, but it takes some guts to do; it's cutting against a lot of our social conditioning to speak out in this way, so as a leader you have to show the courage to keep challenging, and encourage others to do the same. You will have healthier discussions and make better collective decisions as a result.

THE COURAGE TO **CHANGE**

Not every decision you make will be the right one, and that doesn't mean you made it for the wrong reasons either. With disruption knocking on every door, circumstances and information can very quickly change and that means you have to adapt and course-correct as you go along. It may be perceived as a 'flip-flop' by your team but it's far better to admit the error and turn back early than continuing down a dead-end road map while you work out some way to save face and shift the blame. Being wrong and admitting to being wrong doesn't have to be a bad day; it can be a brilliant opportunity to show your honesty and trust in the team, asking for their help in coming up with alternative solutions.

Words of Wisdom: be fearless

We cannot expect comfort along this journey and we can never become complacent. We must be brave and fearless enough to drive the change this world need and support each other as much as we can – as peers, mentors and friends. Women, especially those just getting started, have such an incredible opportunity to bring a new way of thinking and collaborating to the workplace if they show up as their whole selves and have confidence in everything that they have to offer.

HARRIET GREEN – GENERAL MANAGER, IBM WATSON IOT, CUSTOMER ENGAGEMENT AND EDUCATION.

THE COURAGE TO **FAIL**

Not everything is going to go to plan so it's good to recognise early on in your career that getting things wrong is sometimes a necessary step on the way to getting them right. As a leader you're in an exposed position: people are watching your actions and their results; indeed, results are what you will be judged by. But if you obsess over the illusion of a perfect record, you will miss opportunities to experiment, to try new things and to do better in the long run.

All of which means you need to be willing to fail, and be seen to fail. That may seem counter-intuitive, but if you are not getting anything wrong or ever tripping up, then you are playing it too safe. Don't limit yourself to what is known and comfortable. Have the courage to fail, make sure you learn from it when you do, and develop a team ethic that supports people putting themselves outside their comfort zone and learning from their mistakes.

Kindness

Becoming a leader is a brave thing to do, and it often makes you a braver person too. To courage, an obvious leadership asset, we think you need to add another which hasn't always been a big part of the business lexicon. That is kindness.

Many view business as a ruthless, Darwinist world where winner-takes-all and forget everything and everyone else. When profit margins and shareholder value are the aims, there is a certain logic to this. Shoot first, do everything in your power to protect the bottom line, and ask questions later.

Yet, like an increasing number of people, we think that business has the potential to be about so much more than profit. You want to be profitable, of course, but it should be the purpose behind the profit that drives a business forward. Of course shareholders are important, but there are many other stakeholders who are also essential to the long-term success of a business. Moreover, our belief is that business is one of the great global forces for driving innovation that changes lives, transforms opportunities and underpins progress.

Brilliant, mission-driven business leaders are at the heart of global efforts to tackle poverty, deadly diseases, and social and gender inequality. That's not to say business is perfect – any number of corporate scandals can attest to that – but we are entering an era where the collective focus in business has become much more about the positive impact that companies can and should deliver. The revolutionary concept of the 'B-Corp', a certification for businesses that benefit people, community and the planet, and the 2012 launch of Richard Branson's B-Team to champion a better way of doing business are both signs of change and the growing momentum for businesses to have a conscience as well as a capitalist imperative.

In a business world that's more purposeful, more socially aware and conscious of its impact on people and planet, leadership has to change too. Your style needs to reflect the attitudes and ambitions of the people on your team. Which means command and control is out; empathy and kindness are in.

Some will shake their heads at that, and not be persuaded that it is anything other than hippy nonsense. They are entitled to their view, but the importance of kindness to modern leaders is grounded in some important and new realities. Here are two good reasons why you need to be kind to step up and lead today.

WE ARE IN A RELATIONSHIPS AGE; EMPATHY DELIVERS BETTER BUSINESS RESULTS

It's important to recognise that at this time of heightened technological commodification, when there's always a cheaper platform for your customers to choose, the strength of your business lies in the sum and strength of its relationships. From employees to customers, suppliers, investors and observers, a business runs on the quality of its human interactions and the goodwill you build and sustain with your full range of stakeholders.

That has to start with your team. They are the principal ambassadors and spokespeople for the company. They will tell their friends, their social networks and their contacts what sort of place your company is to work in. They will compare notes and assess equivalent opportunities elsewhere. Your people have options aplenty and places to go if they don't like the environment you create. They are as brainy and footsy as you, so invest in developing relationships with them, understand what motivates them and work to fully appreciate their point of view.

PEOPLE NO LONGER RESPECT THE RANK AND UNIFORM

Being an empathetic leader isn't about being a nice boss or wanting to be liked. It's a fundamental part of building strong relationships with your team. You can no longer expect to be listened to purely on the basis of being 'the boss'. You have to earn the respect of your people; and that means you should be listening and learning from them as much as you are talking and giving instructions. Listening is the operative word here! Take the time to listen to people's worries as well as their wild ideas, their criticisms, concerns and, yes, their reflections on your leadership style. Only by listening will you learn what your team needs from you as a leader to help them deliver awesome results.

That doesn't mean you always have to agree with what you hear from others. The important thing is that you take the feedback on board and then, once you've reached a decision, explain clearly why you have chosen that particular course of action. People might disagree with your thinking, but they will generally respect a leader who takes the time to listen, explain and work through their decisions. The alternative is a didactic 'do as I say' style which only feeds disaffection and alienation. That's not something you can afford if you want to avoid losing your best people to another company of their choosing.

Don't think of empathy as a concession to other people; see it for what it is: a vital part of your leadership toolkit, one that helps you build better relationships with your team, empower your people and achieve better outcomes as a result.

Empathy is the oil in the machine, helping avoid misunderstandings that can fester over time into real problems. By making yourself a kinder, more empathetic leader, you will be helping yourself become a better one: someone more in touch with your people, your customers and how your business functions at all levels. Don't think of kindness as a nice-to-have value add; see it as central to your personal and leadership development.

14

Work on your empathy

A big part of stepping up to become a leader is being more aware of how other people respond to you, the things you say and the body language signals you send. It's time to invest in your empathy skills and significantly dial up your self-awareness

Leading with empathy: some scenarios

Before we get into some suggestions and advice on how to develop empathy, let's put you to the test with some scenarios. We'll outline some situations you may encounter as a leader, ask you to think about how you would respond, and then make some suggestions for how an empathetic response might differ from the obvious, instinctive one.

Scenario 1: A performance appraisal with someone you line manage has been moved twice, and now you need to move it a third time because an important client commitment has arisen. How do you handle it?

The instinctive response: The client commitment comes first and I'm busy, so I dash off a quick email to let them know and offer some alternative times. This is an internal meeting we can do at any time; this person is usually in the office so it shouldn't affect them too much. They'll understand that clients always have to come first.

The empathetic response: Moving a one-to-one meeting once is understandable, twice is unfortunate but three times is a problem. Yes, the client commitment comes first, but someone who has been rescheduled this many times is rightly going to feel that they are at the bottom of the pile; I can't afford that. I don't send an email, but make sure to seek them out in person to apologise for the reschedule and to emphasise that we will be getting it back in the diary as soon as possible. When we do meet, I take them out of the office for a coffee, so the conversation is more informal and the meeting feels less routine. I make sure to apologise again for having had to reschedule the meeting so many times.

Scenario 2: An important project team is running into difficulties because of an obvious clash in styles between two key members. Things are becoming increasingly heated and there is obvious ill-feeling. What do you do?

▶

The instinctive response: These people are well-paid grown-ups, they need to sort it out for themselves and learn to live with each other. It's not my job to referee this sort of disagreement, and I haven't got time to get into all the ins-and-outs with them. At most, I call a meeting between the relevant parties to bang heads together and emphasise that I expect them to be professional, and get on with their jobs. End of conversation.

The empathetic response: These are both good people and important team members. A dispute of this sort is inevitably going to impact on all of their work, even beyond the immediate project at hand. I need to do something that will defuse the tension and help get things back on an even keel. I begin by seeing both individually to hear the grievances for myself, and take a view on whether I should try to find a way of making it work, or need to separate the pair for their and everyone else's good. If the decision is to carry on, we agree new ground rules and I check in on their progress. If it's to make a change, I allow some time to pass and find another reason to bring the pair together again, to explore whether their relationship can be healed away from the tension of a high-profile project.

Scenario 3: You are chairing a regular internal meeting, where some members of the team frequently dominate the conversation, where others – though not more junior – tend to speak little. Do you pay any attention?

The instinctive response: It's business as usual, some people are naturally more vocal in meetings and they often come up with good ideas, so there is no benefit in trying to clip their wings. I let things carry on without comment.

The empathetic response: I observe behaviour over a number of weeks to ensure that it is a pattern and not an exception or one-off. If I think that some people in the meeting are holding back from speaking because they do not feel comfortable interjecting themselves into the conversation, I take them aside to informally ask their view, and say I will support them to take a more active role. At subsequent meetings, with their prior knowledge, I make a point of calling on them to contribute.

REFLECTION: Are the scenarios above familiar? Is the more empathetic response something you would naturally take on, or would you follow the instinctive route? Think about instances within your own working life where you could be doing things differently to help people within your organisation address a problem. Identify some areas of the business and individuals you could do more to get to know so you can better understand how you may be able to usefully support them.

THESE SCENARIOS WERE DEVELOPED IN COLLABORATION WITH 360 TRAINING FOR USE AT UNRULYVERSITY

Developing empathy

To some extent, empathy is a human skill that is an inherent part of our social make-up. Yet this vital leadership skill is also one that you can develop, train and hone. Empathy is partly a general mindset around how you treat people, but becoming an empathetic leader is also about techniques that help you understand the signals you are sending to people, and how they are responding. So before we move on, we want to offer some practical tips for how you can work on your empathy skills.

The first thing to understand is that the process of your behaviour is like dropping a stone in a pool. It has ripples, beyond those you might immediately see in the people around you. As a leader, you set the tone for an organisation. You are someone who is carefully watched by all your team, for the smallest signals about when you might be unhappy with their work, worried about some business problem, or disengaged for some other reason. This is not just in the meetings you chair and the emails you send. It is your whole demeanour around the office, your body language and soft signals, so be mindful of your mood and behaviours in the workplace as they can spread like wildfire and you really don't want your bad mood going viral!

Here are some things to think about and coping strategies for becoming a more empathetic leader.

RECOGNISE YOUR OWN REACTIONS

In every conversation and interaction you have, however brief, there is a huge amount of information that is both transmitted and interpreted. You are sending all sorts of signals whether you realise it or not. You need to develop a keen understanding for how the way you react to things affects those around you. Deep and unintentional meaning may be read into something as simple as a rolling of the eyes or raising of the eyebrows. Try and monitor yourself through three lenses:

1   *Verbal reaction* Is your language and choice of words appropriate for the situation?

2   *Non-verbal reaction* How do you come across? Slumped in your chair or sat up and leaning forward? Making eye contact or looking away? Imagine the tables were turned right now – how would you want the person on the other side of the table to behave?

3 *Tonal reaction* The same words can carry very different meanings depending on how you use them. Do you sound like you feel (which will often be rushed, overburdened and irritable) or are you making a conscious effort to moderate yourself to meet a perfectly innocent inquiry or greeting from a colleague on its own terms?

RECOGNISE OTHER PEOPLE'S REACTIONS

As well as examining your own responses, you also need to pay close attention to how the people you are interacting with respond. Here, you need to be very conscious of the gap between verbal expression and non-verbal reaction. People might be saying the things you want to hear, and which they know are expected, but you shouldn't judge on verbal response alone – let's face it, a pursed lip or an eye roll speaks a thousand words.

Take a close look at people's body language. Do they look as engaged and confident as their words suggest? Is there a hint of reluctance, uncertainty or disengagement? Often these will be very subtle signals. It's not always deep sighs and people rolling their eyes. The first flicker of response before anything is spoken often holds the clue to what someone really thinks.

There are many different personality types and presentation styles; no two people will react the same to a request or instruction, and those same people will need different approaches to motivate and encourage them. Praise, for example, is something that some people feed off while others recoil from it, especially in a public setting. And where one person might be mortified by criticism, it might be exactly what another personality needs to focus and motivate them. Past a certain size, your team will be a diverse mix of introverts and extroverts, thinkers and feelers, planners and hackers. A big part of the challenge of leadership is creating an environment that allows all those distinctive styles to find their way and succeed within your team. It's also a big part of what makes it fun!

In the end, there's no substitute for spending time getting to know the people you manage, understanding their style and how you can best engage with them, from briefing on new work, to providing feedback during a project, and rewarding them for success. Some people you'll have a natural rapport with and others you'll need to spend more time getting to know – regardless of how well you think you know someone, it's a good idea to have an up-front conversation with your team members about what they need from you and how you can help them to succeed.

A good rule of thumb is to have regular one-to-one meetings with your team members – at least once a fortnight, ideally more often than that – and to ask them what they need from you, if there's anything you can unblock or anything you should stop doing. And if you don't yet have a team you may well have a boss, so take the opportunity in one-to-one meetings with them to ask what more you could be doing to help them, help their team and help the business. Once you clearly understand what you can do to deliver wow, you're in a much better position to deliver the goods.

Words of wisdom: Leading with empathy

I have noticed two other things that matter in leadership – empathy and execution. Empathy is the ability to think about what really matters to other people. Execution is the ability to turn this into action. Emotion is great, but what matters more is how you channel it into real action. The emerging generation of leaders are more multi-disciplinary which will be so good for innovation. Each job is an opportunity for further growth. However, greatness comes from depth and repetition of task as well. It is about being open to change, being resilient, being tenacious – and all with empathy. Because, let's face it, getting people to do things – especially if not directly reporting to you – is really hard work! We are in the age of selfies, narcissism, post-truth and rapid changes in technology which have empowered you. But now, more than ever, try to see the world through other people's point of view and not just your own.

GERARD GRECH, CEO OF TECH CITY UK

15

Create a culture

Great teams run on great cultures, the essential values and beliefs that underpin how an organisation delivers and works together

To build a successful team, you must also create a successful culture. Great people, led brilliantly, are essential but they are only the start. For businesses of all sizes you need a strong, clearly articulated and vibrant culture.

As a leader, culture reaches the places you cannot. You can't be in every meeting, making every decision and on top of every project. Many things will – and must – happen that you will never see or hear about (unless something goes wrong!), so a core part of your leadership journey will be shaping a culture that can help you do your job when you're not there to do it.

That is something which can be unsettling. Many leaders are personalities who like to have a handle on as much as possible. Yet there is both a benefit and a necessity in letting go. The advantage, as we have discussed, is that you empower your people by trusting them to make decisions and forge their own path. The necessity is simple: beyond a certain size, and in a start-up it happens sooner than you expect, there'll be too much going on for you to be pulling all the levers yourself. This is where culture becomes a powerful part of your leadership toolkit.

What do we mean by culture? At its simplest, culture is a set of shared beliefs and behavioural expectations that an organisation lives and works by. It's not a rulebook, but rather a blueprint – both written and unwritten – that people can use to help them work with colleagues, clients and partners. Think of culture as a common agreement across an organisation on how it seeks to behave and act. Stick a fork in any business and culture is what comes out. Every business has a culture, whether it's good or bad. It's in the policies, prioritisations and processes you develop, and the behaviours and relationships of the people you hire. Company values are where culture starts, but cannot be where it ends. Written-down values and words on a page are not in themselves culture: they fuel and inspire it, but culture is how those good intentions live and grow within your organisation and among your people.

Next we will talk about how you start to shape a culture and values that can be defining for your team, giving you a sense of shared purpose and a guiding star to follow.

Shaping culture

In recent years, the importance of culture, and of start-up culture in particular, has come to the attention of bigger businesses, who see their own place on the FSTE 100 or Fortune 500 threatened by newer companies, with innovative business models and ambitious, can-do cultures. There are 'innovation field trips' to Silicon Valley in California and 'Tech City' in London, as leaders at the very top echelons of the world's most famous brands have the humility, curiosity and foresight look to start-up culture to help them move faster and innovate more. Cultivating a start-up culture – focused on mission and fuelled by empowered employees – is increasingly being seen as a route to building happy, engaged and productive teams, that in turn will deliver better returns for shareholders.

You won't be surprised when we tell you that culture isn't something you can introduce overnight or simply click your fingers and order into being. It doesn't sit on a page and it doesn't grow according to a plan. Culture is the most organic of forces; something that, like a rare flower, can be cultivated, encouraged and nurtured, but will only grow if the conditions are right for it. So the first thing to understand as a leader trying to shape a culture is you can't completely control it; no more than a gardener can control the weather. However, what you can do as a stepping up leader is create the right environment for a positive culture to thrive. Here, based on our experience of fostering start-up and scale-up cultures, are some of the key cultural components to consider.

PURPOSEFUL

Companies with purpose are 400 per cent more profitable than their peers. In the team you lead, you need a purpose that is bigger than a bottom line, one that allows your people to be their bravest selves, do work that challenges the status quo and deliver meaningful impact. Purpose allows you to shape a future and an industry that you and your people want to be a part of. You cannot have a successful culture without a defining purpose, so that's where you need to start.

PEOPLE FIRST

Building a strong culture and nurturing your people first and foremost means you can be confident you've got a committed team prepared to tackle the toughest problems. A company's culture comes to life through its people; they are the custodians of your culture. Every person you recruit to your team will have some impact, big or small, on the overall culture. That means you need to hire with culture in mind, recognise people who best embody the values and be open to the evolution of a culture as the people, size and stage of your team or business change.

OPEN

In times of disruption, an open and transparent culture is more important than ever – you want to know that every member of the team feels comfortable bringing bad news and raising market challenges at an early stage. You also want people who are willing to challenge decisions, and make sure that you have the forums for that to happen. Use all-company Town Halls or regular team meetings to communicate challenges and surface what's NOT working, and give your people the opportunity to break into smaller groups and discuss so it's not just a one-way, top-down broadcast. You need all your people to be using their eyes and ears, so foster an open culture that allows good ideas to come from all quarters – some of our best ideas have come from work experience students and interns, but they'll only share their thoughts if they feel empowered to contribute.

AGILE

Especially in a time of uncertainty, you need your culture to be open to new directions and fundamentally open-minded. If you keep listening, keep learning, keep reading, keep evolving, keep experimenting and keep questioning, you can keep on being at the cutting edge of trends that are reshaping the world we live in. There are so many unknowns and unknown unknowns that it's important to focus on the things you can control, rather than the things you can't. Maybe you can't control what happens in your overall business, but you can have an impact on the team you're a part of. With so much data available, everyone runs the risk of being paralysed by fear and by needing 'just one more data point' before making a decision. The honest truth is that the data points are changing all the time and there'll always be another reason to delay, so make your personal ethos and your team culture agile enough to get on with the job at hand, even under an onslaught of change.

CURIOUS

If your culture is going to be agile enough to respond to a world of constant change, it also needs to be one that has learning at its core. You want an ethos that has curiosity running through its veins, where your people take every opportunity to learn new skills, soak up new ideas and meet new influencers and industry leaders. The best entrepreneurial cultures aren't just about creating an environment for people to do their jobs well: they're about helping them learn about their industry so they end up doing their jobs better.

COLLABORATIVE

In uncertain times, the future can feel like a formidable foe. We all have a better chance of coming out on top if we pool resources and work together to face uncertainty. Within a team that means listening to each other's opinions and playing to individuals' strengths. Internally, that can mean cross-functional crack squads working to solve particular pain points or capitalise on product opportunities. Beyond the walls of a company, it means forging more partnerships and strategic alliances. Don't be a closed circle; always be open to new ideas, new partners and new possibilities.

DIVERSE

It's a simple rule: the more diverse the team, the better the decision making. The more diverse the company, the more innovative it is. And the more diverse your workforce, the greater revenues you'll bring in. A recent report from the consultants McKinsey showed that companies in the top quartile for diversity are 35 per cent more likely to have financial returns above the average for their industry. So make your culture one that doesn't just welcome diversity, but one which also actively champions and facilitates it.

VALUES-CENTRIC

The most important thing for you, as leader, is not even to set the values: it's to live the values. Values are behaviours not statements. Almost all companies past a certain size have statements of mission, purpose and values. Very few live by them. For values to be real, you have to hire and fire by them, promote and demote by them, start and stop projects based on them. And you have to do that consistently, all the time, for a long time. Only then can you earn the right to talk about values and culture.

Action: Organise a Team Summit or set up a Culture Working Group to start exploring what purpose, collaboration, agility and openness could mean in the ▶

context of your team. Along with your colleagues, workshop the following questions:

- What is our mission: the driving central purpose of what we are here to do?
- What do we care about: individually and collectively?
- What are our strengths: the things that make us unique and different?
- What do we do that we love?
- What would we change tomorrow if we could?
- What doesn't work as well as it should? How might we start to change that?
- What is our biggest single goal for the next three months and the next year?

Use the results to create a culture map for your business, which could include:

- The key things you want to achieve together
- Team strengths
- Commitments you will make to each other and the team
- Expectations you have of people joining the team

Words of wisdom: Bringing out the best in people

Leadership is all about bringing out the best in people and it is not about a big ego. It is better not to think that you are the cleverest person in the room. Instead surround yourself with the best and enable them to perform. That way, you achieve what is good for you and good for them. Confidence is important but if you are too confident, you don't try harder. A little bit of insecurity keeps you on your toes!

Never think you are the finished article. Be endlessly curious. Be interested in people. Listen with attention. Think about what is going on around you in the world and how it might affect your business. Your empathetic skills will take you a great deal further than your analytical mind or academic qualifications.

'Turn up on time and follow up' are wise words to live by in your career – and in life! Be reliable, show up, take action. Your ability to hold someone's confidence and to be trusted to deliver – and for that to be right – cannot be underestimated in your journey to the top. Decide what you want to achieve in your work and life – rather than see it as a competition to be better or bigger or richer or more adored than the next person. Be purposeful instead. Set your goals by what really matters for you. The journey may be complicated, unexpected stuff happens along the way, but your life will be more interesting!

ROBERT SWANNELL, CHAIRMAN OF MARKS & SPENCER

Step 4: Votes – on a page

Takeaways

- The team is the most important investment you will make as a leader: focus as much of your energy as you can afford into finding, supporting and championing great people.

▶

- The two abiding qualities of great team leaders are courage and kindness. You need the courage not only to take difficult decisions and be responsible for them, but also to put trust in other people and delegate, to accept when you have got it wrong and need to change, and to keep going even when difficulties pile up.
- Invest in your empathy skills, to build strong relationships with your team in a highly competitive market for talent, and equip yourself with a rounded perspective on the team you lead from all levels.
- Develop greater awareness of your own words, body language and tone, and how they are received by others. Recognise that everyone is different and will need to be treated accordingly.
- Work to establish a written and understood culture: a set of values, principles and purpose that guides your team and its people, providing a blueprint for how to work together and do business.

Assignment

Take one day or a half-day to immerse yourself in the everyday work of someone on your team. Sit with them, work with them and understand how the team and company looks from their perspective. What did you learn that you didn't already know? What would you change as a result?

Read and listen

Books

- Belinda Parmar, *The Empathy Era: women, business and the new pathway to profit,* Lady Geek Ltd 2014

- General Stanley McChrystal and David Silverman, *Team of Teams: new rules of engagement for a complex world,* Portfolio Penguin 2014
- Patrick Lencioni, *The Five Dysfunctions of a Team: a leadership fable,* John Wiley and Sons 2002

Music

- Beach Boys, *Good Vibrations*
- Starship, *We Built This City*
- High School Musical, *We're All in This Together*

Up next

Providing clarity through minimum viable planning, organising people and extreme communication

Navigating uncertainty with a flexible mindset and agile approach

step five

VICTORIES: deliver brilliant results!

We're nearing the end of your stepping up journey. So far we've looked at some of the theory, and plenty of practical applications, behind what it takes to step up to leadership roles in a world that is fast-moving and constantly changing. How you can go from establishing a guiding leadership mission, to building your toolkit of stepping up skills, growing a network and a team around you, and developing the leadership qualities of courage, kindness and empathy.

Now we want to end with a focus on how you make things happen. How you rack up the wins, and achieve the all-important victories that will define your growth as a leader.

Because, if we're being honest, that's what leadership ultimately boils down to: the ability to create the conditions, inspire the actions and hold everything together for long enough to make stuff happen, have an impact and deliver brilliant results.

How do you organise the team, create the necessary processes and respond to changing circumstances on an everyday basis? What processes do you need to put in place, and how much will you need to rely on agility and flexibility? What are the hacks and shortcuts that can ensure you get the best out of your team when the pressure is on and the deadlines are looming?

That's what we'll be looking at on this final step, with a particular focus on the following assets.

Providing clarity

From the way a company communicates, to the way projects and teams are managed, one of the essential assets a leader must bring is clarity. However good the people, a complex project will soon hit the rocks if there isn't sufficient clarity around timelines, roles and priorities. Here we'll look at different ways that, as a leader, you can light the way ahead for your teams as they tackle challenging projects and assignments.

Navigating uncertainty

The flip side of providing clarity is that, as a leader, you will constantly be facing uncertainty, known unknowns and changing circumstances which drop into your inbox unannounced or stream through your social feeds when you're eating breakfast. Having the agility to respond to these changes, and the flexibility to adapt your structures and processes, is one of the key requirements of leaders today.

Wearing many hats

As a leader, what is your role? The answer is you'll need to wear many hats and to constantly change them, as your day-to-day role adapts and flexes to meet the needs of your team and the unpredictable challenges you face.

Words of wisdom: Focus on effort; it's what you can control

Three main ingredients make leaders (and people) successful in this exciting but tumultuous world: Imagination, optimism and courage. Being able to 'see' and get excited about the future is infectious and fun. Having the resilience and

▶

► *determination to see it through makes everyone (including you) successful and happy.*

Most organisations spend all their time focused on the results after they have happened; it can create frustration, panic, short cuts and compromises. Of course good results are super important, but never forget that results lag effort. The more inspired the effort, the better and more satisfying the results. So be the one that identifies and focuses on the effort; it is the only thing that we can control in business.

MIKE KELLY, FOUNDER AND CEO, KELLY/NEWMAN VENTURES

16

Provide clarity

One of your most important roles as a leader is to provide clarity to your people, in planning, project management and communication

What do you want me to do? What's next? Remind me again, why are we doing this? These are the questions you field every day as a leader. Depending on your role and seniority, your team will look to you to provide clarity on company mission and goals, clarity around how people should work together, clarity on the success of projects, and clarity around what's coming next. It's unrealistic to think you can provide certainty in a fast-moving environment, but what you can do is provide as much clarity – of purpose, process and priorities – to your team as you are capable of.

As a leader, your commitment to clarity should be focused on three specific areas that are essential to get right: planning workstreams, organising people and communicating objectives and outcomes, so that your team know what victory looks like.

Minimum viable planning

Whatever project, launch or initiative you're trying to deliver with a team, you'll need a plan. That doesn't mean you should sit down and write a planning document that rivals *War and Peace*, or build a 10,000 cell GANTT chart that maps out a project inch-by-inch over a period spanning months. In today's business environment that would be commercial suicide and a waste of time that you simply can't afford.

Instead, what it means is compiling a crowd-sourced skeleton plan to provide a constant yardstick and reference point for the lifetime of a project. In the same vein as the minimum viable product (a term which refers to the simplest version of a product that you launch with), you need a minimum viable plan for projects: the simplest plan possible that will get your team aligned around what you're trying to achieve, who's doing what and when it needs to be delivered.

You should get started by bringing the project team together as soon as possible and holding a kick-off meeting where you in your role as leader start by giving the commercial context of the project – why we're doing this and why we're doing it now – and set out any top-level goals you want the project to deliver, e.g. new clients, more website traffic, improved deal conversion . . . of course, this will be different for each and every project. Once you've done that, you can open a shared document and write the MVP together. It should include the following:

- **Context:** Why are we doing this project? What's the business rationale and is there a reason it's especially important now?

- **Goals:** What are we seeking to achieve and deliver? On launch, post-launch? What does good/better/best look like on this project?

- **Timing:** How long will it take and can we chunk delivery into phases?

- **People:** Who's the executive sponsor, the project manager, key stakeholders, and who assumes ownership of specific areas? Are we missing anyone we need to make this happen?

- **Resources:** What's the budget; do we need additional space, people, co-funding?

- **Obstacles:** What could slow us down or trip us up? Any lessons that we want to remember from previous projects? Anything we can do to pre-empt this from happening ahead of time?

- **Next steps:** What are the very next steps that need to happen – with a name against each one? Is there anyone not here who needs to know about the project and when will we next meet to discuss progress? (Establishing a project email alias or slack channel on day one can massively help streamline communications.)

It's important to note that the minimum viable plan does not map out step by step everything that needs to happen over the lifetime of the project; it's a compass rather than a map and that's a key distinction as it builds resilience, agility and flexibility into the project from the outset, whilst at the same time bringing absolute clarity as to the purpose, process and people involved in delivery.

As well as building the beginnings of a living plan, writing the document together ensures the whole group is bought into the project and understands WHY the project is important. If you can explain the purpose of the workstream, the team can be more valuable contributors to the project. Co-writing an MPV together will also help you start to shape a committed team of people who understand their roles and take responsibility for ownership of the plan and the project's success.

Use the MVP as your shared agenda for subsequent group meetings, so you can keep track of actions in the context of your original goals and be explicit with the team as and when things need to change, which they undoubtedly will!

When you're the leader responsible for delivering ongoing workstreams that may not warrant a project plan, you should still consider how you bring clarity to the team around workflow planning. That might mean a longer planning session every fortnight where a team agrees priorities, supplemented by 15-minute daily stand-up meetings, where everyone shares an update on yesterday's progress, today's focus and potential blockers. By getting all the people together briefly, and the information on the table, you can troubleshoot in real time, avoid duplication of effort and surface opportunities to shortcut.

Tip: Do as few meetings sitting down as you can. Emphasise brevity and maintain momentum by doing status meetings on your feet. If you're leading the group, don't forget to ask whether there any blockers you can help with – this is the chance for your teams to flag any issues with you.

A meeting such as this can be organised either via Trello, a project management app, or for a low-tech alternative, with Post-it notes on a physical wall. Mark up key tasks with the name of the person owning them, and include timings such as 'Upcoming', 'To do this week', 'To do today', or 'Done'. The wall then becomes a live representation of the status of a team's workstreams and a visual marker of progress and the work yet to come. It also makes everyone on the team publicly accountable for what they have said they'll deliver.

As you step up and take control of multiple projects and teams, these MVP templates come in very handy and help you to scale best planning practices across your business. Not everything will run smoothly, though, and continuous learning and adaptation of processes is a key part of the leader's responsibility, especially when teams come together for the first time and may have different styles and approaches.

As a leader, you need to have a mindset of continuous improvement: every significant undertaking by your team should be throwing up new ideas and thinking for the business to assimilate and build on. Start to see planning as a vital ingredient in developing your team's collective knowledge and skill base.

Action: Can you spot an opportunity to try an MVP approach? Let the team know it's an experiment and prepare a template with questions in advance so you can hit the ground running when the meeting starts. Work hard to include everybody's point of view. Assign a scribe to capture next steps. At the end of the session, which could be as long as two hours, ask yourself the following:

● Are the goals clearly defined and is the timeline agreed?

▶

- Does everyone on the team know exactly what their role and key responsibility is? Is there anyone not in that meeting, maybe a peer from another team or your boss, who should be on the email alias and given access to the MVP so they have visibility of the project?
- Are there any areas of confusion that you as a leader need to go away and address, e.g. secure additional budget or check alignment with company goals?

Sarah says: Start at the end

The first thing that happens at the beginning of an Unruly project is that a retrospective is booked into the diary for the end of the assignment, to collectively discuss how things went, what we learned and what we would consider doing differently the next time. The phrase 'post-mortem' is banned because this is not about apportioning blame or focusing on shortcomings. Rather, it's about ensuring that the work just completed is recognised, celebrated and acts as a springboard for the next big project, and that the vital intelligence gained in the heat of a high-intensity assignment is not lost but captured and put to good use for the future.

Just as there is a temptation to skimp on the planning of new projects, it is easy to fall into the bad habit of shifting focus and moving on from a project the moment the ribbon is cut on a new product, or the launch you were planning is out of the way. Don't miss out on the opportunity to learn from all the work that has been put in. Make retrospectives a key part of how you learn from big projects and apply learnings to future work.

And don't allow retrospectives to become a blame game. Start each of these meetings with a statement of the 'prime directive', a central part of the Agile development ethos: *'Regardless of what we discover, we understand and truly believe that everyone did the best job they could, given what they knew at the time, their skills and abilities, the resources available, and the situation at hand.'* The statement is invaluable to setting a positive and non-judgemental tone.

Organising people

We've already discussed the importance of nurturing and developing the individual members of your team; if you want to secure the victories, it's just as important that people are organised to best effect. Think of your team not just as specialist individuals organised according to specific skills and workflow, but also as a group of people that will need to be mobilised in different ways at different times to have the maximum impact. Here are some key ways to do that.

PAIRS

One of the most effective ways of organising people is to pair them up. This is a technique often used in software development, where two people writing code together – although it may seem slower – will be more efficient in the long term than solo actors. As a pair, developers can peer-review each other's code in real time and come up with better solutions when they're pairing on the code base. Mistakes are spotted and corrected before the code goes live and knowledge of the code base doesn't live in just one person's head.

This is something you can apply well beyond software. A team of two means there's someone to bounce ideas off, play the devil's advocate, and to proofread, fact check (or sanity check!) each other's work. Work at pairing together people with contrasting skills and personalities, who will improve each other and produce better work together than they could alone. Encourage your pairs to deepen their partnership in other ways, presenting at conferences, for instance.

MOBS

The practice of 'mobbing' takes pairing to another level. This is where you bring together the full muscle of a team to attack a big problem or open up discussion of a new area as one big group. In software development, it means a group of engineers sitting around one super-sized screen for up to an hour, each taking turns at the keyboard, working on the same piece of code. It's a brilliant way of making sure that thought processes and knowledge bases are shared across a wider group. It's a practice you can apply to all parts of your team, from HR to marketing: get a mob together to contribute to the same piece of work, provide feedback and build on ideas in real time. This can even work for teams based across different offices and helps to massively reduce information asymmetry. Are there any projects you're running in your company that you think would benefit from a mobbing session? They're exhilarating, positive, shared experiences that can generate unexpected ideas and give a whole team a stronger sense of ownership.

SQUADS

In addition to pairs and mobs, for large projects consider creating squads: cross-functional teams that bring together people from all areas of the business to collaborate on key projects such as a new product or major campaign launch.

A squad can vary in size, depending on how many different teams need to be across a project. Together they develop a minimum viable plan and meet regularly to discuss progress.

On the road to victory, squads fulfil a number of purposes:

- **To signal the importance of the project** As special teams that have been brought together specifically for a given assignment, they help increase focus and purpose around the project at hand and the rest of the company can also see that this is a priority area.

- **To solve complex business challenges** Squads are designed as crack teams that are first and foremost about bringing together all the necessary skills and experience to deliver on complex projects. By being cross-functional across all areas of the business, they bring a range of different perspectives and necessary skill sets to certain problems. For the same reason, they serve to spread interest and awareness of key projects company-wide, and to represent the needs (and concerns) of all different teams.

- **To help emerging leaders gain cross-functional experience and company profile** Squads can be immensely valuable vehicles for learning and development. With emerging leadership talent, they can offer a proving ground for those ready to gain their first management experience, in an environment where they have more experienced leaders who can have their back and help them keep the show on the road.

Action: Work at mixing up the way your team works and the combinations of people and talent you put on particular projects. That could be encouraging individuals who wouldn't normally work together to take on a joint project, or creating your own multi-skilled 'squad' to tackle a big project or business problem. Create a sense of aspiration around special teams that people should want to become a part of.

Extreme communication

A key part of providing clarity across your team is communication. And while that may sound obvious, the reality is that communication is not just one of the most important parts of any business, it's also one of the most frequently neglected.

Communication is often asymmetrical, in that leaders think they are doing plenty of it, while their people think they are hardly sharing anything at all. As a leader, you need to continually test and challenge your assumptions on how you communicate key business information to your team. Quickly consider these questions:

- Is important (non-confidential or privileged) information regularly shared with the whole team?

- Are key decisions being explained in the context of why and for what reasons they were made?

- Is bad news – e.g. client losses or product defects –
  openly shared and communicated?

The reason communication matters so much is that a lack of consistent information flow from leaders creates a vacuum that is inevitably filled with speculation and rumour. When this happens, it's often more a case of bad organisation than bad intentions. With so much going on, it's incredibly easy to miss things and to allow gaps to appear between the information held at the leadership level and things that are known across the business.

Tip: Try and put yourself in the shoes of the people receiving your communications in order to minimise the scope for communication breakdowns. How will they feel? What will they think and what will they do next? And never be afraid of repeating yourself. Are your people bored of hearing you say the same thing? Excellent news. Your message has finally landed!

When it comes to sharing information, the need to explain context is often overlooked – if you want to step up your communication skills, one easy hack is to start every communication by explaining why. Why you're asking for this now, why the priorities have changed, why you're considering changing the process, why the client has asked to do things differently. The more insight you can communicate here, the more people will understand what you're shooting for and that will put them in a much stronger position to help you succeed and resolve problems with solutions you hadn't even considered. And when your own Big Boss asks YOU to get something done (whether that's your board, your boss or your biggest client), take the time to ask them why they want it, what good looks like and when this needs to be done, so that you in turn are best positioned to deliver wow.

Sarah says: Extreme communications

There's no one 'best' way to communicate across a business, especially as it scales, so if you want to lead the way in communications, you'll want to build a wide range of tools in your communication toolkit. At Unruly we started a weekly newsletter – *The Friday Flash* – when there were only twelve of us in the business and we were all sat on two banks of desks. Over the years it has become indispensable for ensuring that everybody knows what has happened across the business that week. We communicate quarterly objectives orally at Town Hall, by email and also visually with posters on fridges and the backs of toilet doors. Face to face is the best way of sharing information and gauging responses, and if you can do a video hangout rather than a phone call, so much the better! This will help you more effectively read and empathise with your colleague halfway round the world and will help to build the open communication and strong relationships you need as you're stepping up your leadership responsibilities.

To facilitate both information sharing and a two-way dialogue around key decisions, we have a whole series of different forums that bring our teams together, some on a regular pulse and others on an ad hoc basis. As you read through the list, have a think which ones would be the most useful in the context of your own business context. They include:

- Daily 15-minute stand-up meetings to do a quick runaround on progress and key actions (and every Monday, a similar meeting for the whole office)
- Weekly leadership meetings of the exec team and daily 10-minute check-ins

- Fortnightly product planning sessions: these bring together people from across the business to map priorities and resourcing in the engineering team
- Monthly show and tells, where squads and functional teams share latest work, recent findings, changes to process or examples of best practice
- Quarterly exec retrospectives where the exec team meets with a broader senior leadership team to share feedback on the quarter that's gone and to discuss priorities for the quarter ahead
- Quarterly Town Halls where overall company strategic priorities are shared and discussed
- Quarterly #Oneruly days: a 24-hour, all-company #hackathon where every team in the company focuses on a specific strategic objective. This really brings everyone together and can help build massive momentum around important projects
- Annual 'Dragons' Nest' pizza and prosecco events for the team to pitch new product ideas and concepts to the leadership
- Biennial 'UnrulyFests': part training power-up, part knees up! In London, with every employee around the globe on the invite list

Given Unruly now operates across 20 offices and eight different time zones, you can understand the need for rigour in making sure that key messages, developments and achievements are being communicated across the group. Yet the same principle applies even if you are leading a small team who all work within earshot of each other. Proximity is no guarantee of good communication, so you have to work at it, ensuring that people on your team get the opportunity both to understand what's

▶

going on outside their ambit, and to feed in their own ideas into the bargain.

Small things can make a big difference: we do a lot of video hangouts with our international teams, so we had a 'tapered table' built in the boardroom, with video screens at the wide end, to put the people via video at the head of the table, able to see the faces of everyone sitting in the room. This makes remote participants feel more included and has massively increased their active participation in discussion and decision making.

Words of wisdom: Over-communicate your vision

Lead with a vision. Leaders show people a vision for the future and how they can contribute to that. Err on the side of over-communicating your vision. You must ensure everyone knows where and when to point their oar and help row in the right direction. Listen more than you speak. From a social and cultural perspective, listening shows empathy, which is a great trait for leaders to have. But also from a pure business perspective, listening instead of speaking will gather you more data points to make better decisions. Active listening demonstrates that you are aware, respectful of others and above all, coachable – a trait that will serve you well in your career and in life.

ANGIE CHANG, SERIAL ENTREPRENEUR

The leader needs to be transparent and explain the context for decisions – to empower their management team with the knowledge they need to get everyone in the business on board. The leader is someone who can bring a team together. Not just an Exec/Board Team but senior leadership teams. Someone who focuses on people's strengths rather than pulling people up on their weaknesses. I admire leaders that inspire and drive change. With the world moving so fast you can't be left behind. All the leaders I've respected have cool heads and kind hearts.

LOUISE TULLIN, VP MARKETING AND COMMUNICATIONS, EMEA AT UNRULY

Wisdom box:

As a leader, having a clear vision for your business is not enough. Make your vision come alive for your teams through storytelling that creates a picture so that everyone understands not just what role they play, but how that fits into the overall vision. Change is the norm - so get used to it and get your people used to it.

NICOLE SHEFFIELD, CHIEF DIGITAL OFFICER, NEWS CORP AUSTRALIA

17

Navigate uncertainty

As a leader you need to acknowledge the reality of constant uncertainty, prioritise experimentation and build resilience into your people and processes

If one of your key roles as a leader is to give your people the clarity and confidence that provides a licence to operate, an equal and opposite requirement is to deal with the climate of uncertainty that you will face. You'll have to expect the unexpected and deal with situations for which no amount of organisation or planning can prepare you. That's where developing an adaptive mindset, emphasising an action bias and fostering collaborative problem-solving will give you and your team a clear competitive advantage in uncertain times, enabling you to act quickly while other leaders, teams, companies and organisations dither, panic or wait out the storm, paralysed by fear of the unknown.

Words of wisdom: Be ready to manage the unexpected

The qualities that I associate with great leaders and great leadership are vision, values, judgement, drive and influence. An ability to drive growth and nurture talent, strong principles demonstrated in words and deeds, a willingness to confront issues boldly, a capacity for fairness, truthfulness, humanity, humility – an obsession with colleagues and customers.

We are operating in uncertain times so emerging leaders have to be ready to anticipate and manage the unexpected, be agile, imaginative and robust in dealing with change. I was taught pretty early on in my career that 'business is about relationships'. Those relationships with colleagues and customers can produce transformational work and great results under the right leadership.

CILLA SNOWBALL, GROUP CHAIRMAN AND GROUP CEO OF AMV BBDO

An ability to acknowledge and navigate uncertainty is at the heart of modern leadership. Yes, make a plan that sets a mission, guiding principles and a time-frame for achieving your goals. But how you get there will be a matter for constant iteration and reinvention.

An element of managed chaos is the reality for many of today's leaders and that's something you need to embrace as a leader.

It means you can never have all the answers, and you should embrace that too. Your role is not to be omniscient, but to have the courage to embrace uncertainty and equip your team to do the same. In today's fast-moving market, far better to be a growth hacker than a monument builder.

All the careful planning in the world cannot anticipate hidden icebergs and unforeseen developments. What do we mean by that? Well, if the first part of effective leadership is the ability to make and shape a plan, the second is to know when you need to rip it up. Sometimes, circumstances will simply dictate that your course of action has been blown off course; and at that stage you may need to intervene with a change of plan.

Do think carefully before you blow your team off course – ask yourself whether you're overreacting to one new data point. Ask yourself whether you've been here before in a similar situation. Ask yourself whether there are alternatives you haven't considered. Ask yourself whether there's anyone else you should talk to who could help you make a better decision. And if you ask yourself all these questions and continue to believe that a change in plan or strategy is needed, then it's time to talk to your team, explaining to them why the change has come about, being clear about what it means for them and their current projects, and asking for their feedback and suggestions for how to make the change a success.

You shouldn't aim to be a chaotic leader, but you must accept that you are leading in what is often a chaotic world; don't let external macroeconomic uncertainty or internal organisational processes stand in your way of making swift decisions and changes when they become necessary. If you want to inspire your team to embrace change, the best way to that is to lead by example.

Many changes will be beyond your control and cannot be averted or prevented – an acquisition, a new market entrant, or economic recession. But you can be mentally and culturally prepared for change by building resilience into your people and processes. Try to work with short planning cycles, allowing you to shift priorities if the market moves around you. And while you may still want to set people quarterly objectives, be prepared that these will likely have to change: that's fine, as long as you explain why the change is happening, and make sure you're de-prioritising other workstreams to allow time to focus on the new priorities. You don't want to be simply piling on additional responsibilities as that will dilute focus and demotivate your team.

In our experience, once people understand that you are thinking through the impact of change and considering how it will affect them, they'll be much more willing to embrace the change and focus on the best ways to make it work.

Context-switching or changing direction mid-project can be especially distracting and demotivating when it affects an entire team, so if priorities do change it's important you explain why. Let your team know what's driven the change in direction, acknowledge that this will affect their outputs and ask for their suggestions on how to best manage the impact and build momentum for the new direction quickly. Here are some proactive strategies for helping you lead through change and uncertainty.

SHARE INFORMATION

When an unexpected change occurs, everyone can feel blind-sided. As leader, you can respond by sharing the information you know. The more information you can share on what happened and why, and what the next steps are, the more you can start to alleviate anxiety produced by shocks and major change events. It helps everybody to know that someone is taking responsibility, and your people will get behind you and support your attempts to regain a sense of equilibrium. If you don't have any information to share, then let people know that you don't have the information to share yet, but that you are going to find it out. In moments of uncertainty or calamity it's very reassuring for people to hear from their leader, and to get a sense of how you are responding. A vacuum of information creates anxiety, and unhelpful rumours creep in to fill the gaps. More often than not, the change is not as dramatic as people might fear, so having regular update meetings will help. You are not alone; you can bring your team together to discuss, to seek opinions, to brainstorm ideas for how to keep moving forward.

PRIORITISE

Don't try to do everything at once. When events are in flux, it doesn't make sense to try to control or respond to everything. Prioritise. Focus on what is most important to tackle first, and next, and third. Allow yourself to feel okay with ambiguity and feeling out of control for a period. Sometimes events need to run their course and they settle down after a few days. Sometimes you have to react fast, and sometimes the best reaction is to wait until it is the right time to act. As you continue to gain experience and confidence in major change situations, the more your instinct grows on how to respond.

ENJOY THE ADRENALIN RUSH

Let's be realistic. The fast pace of change in the world, accelerated in a large part by new digital advancements, is the new normal. So, you may as well hop on board and enjoy the rush! Get comfortable with feeling uncomfortable. Be relaxed about yet another major change event. The more you realise that unpredictability is the new predictability, then you can just let go and liberate yourself from having to be in control all the time. Don't see 'leading through change' as an event that will pass. See it as the new normal and make peace with that.

Perhaps you could set some personal boundaries for yourself so that you enjoy the rush but are not hyper-alert as this would lead to burn out. You don't have to be 'switched on 24/7'. Perhaps you could walk to work, breathe fresh air, look at the sky and learn how to pace yourself to cope with a business that moves so quickly.

STAY PURPOSE-DRIVEN

In turbulent times, it is more important than ever to stay driven by your leadership purpose. When we are tested by change, our purpose can provide us with a steadiness and steadfastness. After all, who you are, why you want to lead and how you want to lead, remain constant. With a strong sense of core purpose, you will know how to react and how to respond, and how to continue to lead regardless of what is happening around you. Without purpose, you are just swaying this way and that, at the mercy of the events rather than staying the course on what you set out to do.

KEEP MOVING FORWARD AND KEEP COMMUNICATING

Sometimes it may feel like you are not making any progress. However, at those most difficult moments, be resilient and don't give up. Keep going. Just put one foot in front of the other, and keep going. Tell yourself that no effort is wasted and you will turn a corner soon. If you give up, it is over. But if you keep trying, there is a chance for progress. Entrepreneurs have a lot to teach leaders of corporations about the challenges of trying to make things happen and get a result. This kind of entrepreneurial intelligence – resourcefulness, pure dogged determination – is the kind of tenacity that is required during testing times of change. Remember to keep communicating and bringing others along with you. You can't do this alone!

KEEP PERSPECTIVE!

When we're very close to events and in a challenging situation, it can be hard to keep a sense of perspective and see the bigger picture. We can create negative downward spirals, when, for example, a pessimistic outlook leads to reluctance to take risk and we retrench rather than expand our range of possibilities. Life is not plain sailing. No matter where you work or what your role, there will be good days and bad days. Resilience is about keeping perspective and mastering the ability to helicopter above the situation and realise that it may not be as bad as you first thought. If you suffer a setback, you can learn from the situation, chalk it down to experience and realise that you're not the first one or the only one who's had to bounce back from a difficult situation. You've got this!

Action: In the role you're in right now, what is your biggest opportunity to have a positive impact on your team or business? Now make a list of three things you currently do that you or your team could stop doing in order to free up time for experimenting with the bigger, higher impact opportunity you've just identified. Better still, workshop this exercise with your team and you may find you have more time than you thought to try something new.

Sarah says: Growth hacking

A great mindset for helping to navigate change is growth hacking. Technically speaking, this refers to the rapid, real-time experimentation, iteration and development of marketing approaches to build and engage a customer base. A growth hacking mentality is about being alive to opportunities to take your business forward, especially those that fall outside the day-to-day routine and those that can have an outsized impact with minimal spend and within a short space of time.

One of my favourite growth hacks is from the early days of Unruly, in 2010, when we were a small start-up of 20 people. The Government was launching its Tech City initiative to promote the London digital start-up scene and the Prime Minister, David Cameron, was hosting an event in East London with the great and good of the tech world in attendance.

Given we were hardly known at that point, unsurprisingly we didn't make it on to the invite list. So we invited ourselves. Specifically, our team stood outside the venue, holding Unruly-branded cushions, as the VIPs filed past us for the launch. Half of them thought we were picketing the event, and the other half that we were the official sponsors! The stunt had the desired effect; we made lots of incredible contacts and got on to the 6pm news that evening. All for an investment that cost us no more than our time.

Three years after our stunt, we were a bigger, better known business. And when Tech City came to launch their signature Future 50 programme, they came to our offices to host the event. We had gone from being the upstart on the outside of the big launch, to being very much on the inside.

Whatever your size and reputation, you can make an impact. Being part of a big company where you have

▶

access to big budgets may feel like an advantage, but sometimes it can stifle imagination and lead to overly cautious decision making. Being resource-constrained forces careful prioritisation and often leads to better and less obvious results. We believe that imagination trumps big budgets and with a clear ambition and eye for an opportunity, you can go a long way on your wits alone. And that's what growth hacking is really all about.

Championing innovation

The most effective way to build resilience into your leadership ethos and at the same time to future-proof your business is through enabling, encouraging and in fact *expecting* innovation and experimentation within your teams.

As a stepping up leader, see your role as setting an example to the rest of the team: the quest for new and better ways of delivering wow shouldn't be an interesting sideline, but a central part of how the entire team thinks and acts. And if that quest involves a fair amount of wrong turns and false dawns, that's fine! Innovation is by its nature speculative, exploratory and likely to fail, so there'll be plenty of ideas that don't work out.

Your role up front is to help filter the new ideas so the ones that get developed are aligned with the team's mission and goals. Next, you'll need to make sure that people's time is freed up to experiment and you'll want to help your team set KPIs (key performance indicators) against the test before it gets underway. Once it gets going, encourage a rapid feedback cycle so that you and the rest of the team can make suggestions and observations that will give the experiment a better chance of success. Finally, regardless of the outcome, recognise the importance of continuous innovation, celebrate the effort that's been put in and disseminate the learnings as broadly as possible so that team members feel motivated and empowered to keep on exploring new opportunities.

Equally, there are some approaches and techniques which can help minimise the risk and maximise the outcomes of new experiments. Here are some suggestions for how you can step up innovation in your team and in doing so build up your reputation within your business as an innovator – someone who recognises and capitalises on the opportunities afforded by new technologies and platforms.

BUILD FROM THE MIDDLE

Don't take the approach that every new idea needs to be lovingly built up, brick by brick from the bottom, like a medieval cathedral. There simply isn't time for that. By the time you're ready for the topping out ceremony, the market will already have moved on.

Forget starting with foundations and instead begin in the middle. Don't waste three months making and positioning the cornerstone; build the altar and see whether people will rally to it. What that means in practice is you need to start at the heart of the problem you're trying to solve, or the opportunity you want to unlock. Whether that's raising awareness of your business in a new market or building a new app to give your customers a better mobile experience, try and identify the nub of the issue: how you could most quickly do something that demonstrates the idea is worth taking further.

The key thing is to test your riskiest assumption as early as possible – before you waste time adding bells and whistles. When market conditions are changing so quickly, and time and money are precious resources, it's much better to fail fast than to fail slowly.

People often ask us, how do you know if you've failed or not? Sometimes it can be difficult to tell, especially when you're in the thick of it. That's why it's critical to be data driven here as there's always a temptation to be swayed by how strongly you feel about an idea or a project. So set clear metrics for what constitutes good/better/best before you start the test and before you get emotionally attached to the project – this will keep you honest!

TEST, LEARN AND TEST AGAIN

With new ideas and experiments, you're often best served by starting small. Test your ideas at limited scale, in just one market or for just one type of customer so you get to the result faster, so you can A/B test how your experiment performed versus what was there already, and so you contain any unforeseen issues without affecting the whole customer base. Based on what you learn, once you've proved out an idea on a small scale, this gives you the case study to go big with the idea. You'll be much more likely to convince your boss and stakeholders to restructure the ops team/use a new analytics provider/crowd-source your weekly agenda if you've piloted the idea on a small scale first and ironed out the kinks.

Don't labour over new experiments. Focus on getting something done, and not making it perfect first time around. See how it goes and most importantly what you can learn. Then refine your approach, try again and see how the results differ. Think of experimentation as many low-cost, low-risk test runs that help you to understand whether there's a worthwhile idea to pursue and, if so, how you can best develop it at larger scale.

CREATE SPACES TO INSPIRE
CREATIVITY AND SAFETY

To keep your team grounded when so much is changing can be a challenge. As you foster your culture of continuous innovation and collaboration, think what you could do with the physical spaces in your workplace to give people room to meet and share ideas. For me, the kitchen table is the most important piece of furniture in the office, and the most important office appliance is not the printer, it's the coffee machine. It's so important to have a space where people can eat together, slurp tea together, dream up ideas together and troubleshoot together in a space that feels safe, a place where they feel encouraged to be themselves, rather than a formal boardroom where people tend to be less natural, more on their guard and as a result less able to think creatively and behave empathetically. If you're part of a smaller company, this space doesn't have to be within your office; it could be a park bench round the corner where you eat a packed lunch and feed the ducks together; it could be a coffee shop where you all feel relaxed and are more likely to come up with a name for that new product you've been stewing over.

And if you don't have a team or you have limited influence over your workspace, don't let that stop you – think about your own desk and how you could hack that square metre of space to become a conversation starter that supports the goals of the organisation. My own desk has a row of favourite business books so I can lend them to people really easily. Our dev team has their walls filled with memes and photoshopped images, the sales team likes to scrawl the week's wins on a white board, and the design team has a wall of nerf guns ready to shoot. What could you do to make your own desk or your team's bank of desks a talking point that inspires conversation and creative thinking within your company?

USE RITUALS TO MAINTAIN A STEADY PULSE

When the political climate is so febrile, your industry is in a state of constant flux, and your business model is being reinvented around you every day, it's easy for things to feel out of control and that's the last thing you want to feel as a stepping up leader.

Focus on the things you can control and keep a steady pulse where possible. Whether it's Monday stand-ups or Friday beers, weekly one-to-ones or exec open hours, regular pub quizzes or quarterly Town Halls, rituals ensure that there's a framework, a scaffold that underpins the activity that's going on.

Sarah says: Nothing's gonna stop us now

At Unruly, we've found that music is a powerful tool for strengthening team rituals, as well as being a great way to create a positive atmosphere. Music in the gym has long been the norm; as you're honing your leadership muscles I'd definitely recommend using music to raise your energy levels, motivate your team and create memorable rituals. First thing on a Monday morning, at the Unruly All Hands stand-up, the UK office is called to the meeting point by the distinctive tones of either Bob Marley (*Get Up, Stand Up*), Ben E. King (*Stand By Me*) or One Direction (*Stand Up*) ringing out across the office.

At the Ops team stand-up meeting on a Friday morning, in addition to our staple Friday stand-up questions – can you share one thing you learnt this week and one challenge you're aware of going into the weekend? – we have a wildcard question, which is often music related: 'What's your favourite song this week?' or 'Name a piece of music that's moved you'. We then make a shared Spotify playlist, where everyone adds the song they've chosen and listens

---

to the playlist on a Friday afternoon. It's often motivational music that helps us power through the final hours of the working week and creates a talking point for the team over Friday beers.

When I asked Unrulies to suggest some tracks for a #SteppingUp playlist, the shared document was flooded with 150+ suggestions in minutes – and you've seen a selection of those choices listed at the end of each chapter. Music tastes are notoriously subjective so you may well prefer to create your own playlist, but in case you find yourself in need of some ready-to-play inspiration, the extended #SteppingUp playlist lives on Spotify.

We've talked a lot in this book about the pace of change and how you need to embrace that to step up as a leader. But that doesn't mean you have to do everything at breakneck speed. The need for speed is becoming a business truism, but in many cases it's the more patient leader who is best placed to assess and take advantage of opportunities. You want a balance between managing fast and slow, between stepping up to act and stepping back to pause and reflect, so be careful not to rush at opportunities just because they're there.

Sometimes the best decisions are those made when you've had a little time to reflect, rather than charging straight into something. You can be too early to markets, products and deals. Pick the races you want to run in carefully. Sometimes it's OK to be the one who hangs back for a better view while everyone else is going hell for leather.

In a business world full of hares, there can be an advantage sometimes (though certainly not always!) in being the tortoise. Sustained effort, combined with patient determination, very often wins the race.

Stepping up to lead really is a marathon not a sprint, and in this book, with its focus on vision, values, velocity, votes and victories, you have the framework you need to prepare you mentally for the challenge. You have the wise words of today's successful business leaders ringing in your ears like a passionate coach, willing you on to win from the sidelines. You have a broad range of tried and tested actions to help you flex your leadership muscles and practise behaviours that will give you the confidence and the skills to truly unlock your leadership potential and step up to the challenges of leadership with authenticity, purpose and empathy. It's time to get on your way!

Step 5: Victories – on a page

Takeaways

- Provide the maximum level of clarity to your team, through effective team and project management and constant communication.
- Have a minimum viable plan, agreed at the outset, where context, goals, timeline, possible landmines, roles, responsibilities and next steps are agreed and recorded.
- A team of two will almost always outperform an individual; so pair up! For more complex projects, build cross-functional squads that can bring together the best of your business in one team for a specific purpose.
- Never stop communicating, because however much leaders think they are communicating, it's rarely perceived as being enough. Don't allow a vacuum to emerge that will be filled with rumour and speculation.

- If circumstances change, you need to be willing to rip up the plan or tweak as needed. Several times. And in real time. There are many forces beyond your control, which will require unexpected U-turns and course changes.
- Put innovation at the heart of your leadership ethos, provide a physical environment where people are inspired to collaborate and create, and use rituals to create a steady pulse.

Assignment

At the end of the next project you're managing, hold a retrospective with everyone involved. Discuss what went well, how they felt at various stages in the project and what you've learned for next time. Work together on a list of learnings that you can put into practice for the next similar project.

Read and listen

Books

- Eric Ries, *The Lean Startup: how constant innovation creates radically successful businesses,* Portfolio Penguin 2011
- Jessica Livingston, *Founders at Work: stories of startups' early days,* Springer 2011
- Kent Beck, *Extreme Programming Explained: embrace change,* Addison-Wesley Professional 2004

Music

- Queen, *Don't Stop Me Now*
- Survivor, *Burning Heart*
- K'NAAN, *Wavin' Flag*

Appendix 1
Checklist: the cheat sheet

A quick recap of some of the main ideas and principles in this book:

- **Embrace the possibilities of change:** With the business world more uncertain than ever before, there is more opportunity than ever to forge a fast path to the top. You don't have to wait around anymore to dutifully climb the ranks; instead, seize the opportunity to make yourself an expert in an emerging field and become the go-to person if you want to accelerate your leadership journey.

- **Go looking for new ideas:** The essence of leadership is the quest for knowledge. You should never stop learning and your curiosity for new ideas should never be sated. Take every opportunity you can to read up, hear experts and immerse yourself in the major trends and technologies affecting your industry. Put yourself in the vanguard of change.

- **Set yourself a leadership mission:** Before you can become a successful leader, you need to discover within yourself why you want to lead and what impact you want to make. Establish a personal leadership mission that can shape and guide your career through any number of different roles and organisations.

- **Make sure you love what you do:** Leadership is a tough road and the only way you are going to make it is if you love what you do, and have a passion that can sustain you through the difficult moments. Choose carefully where you go to build your leadership career and who you take on the journey: whether that's in someone else's company or one you create yourself.

- **Don't wait to be asked:** No one is going to help shape your leadership career for you. If you wait for others to make the running, you could be waiting a long time, so have the confidence and self-belief to put yourself forward for new responsibilities and make suggestions for how things could be done differently. Take control of your own future and shape it in a way that suits and rewards you.

- **Be all about the team:** A great team is what will make you into a great leader. It is the people around you who will save you from pitfalls, keep up your energy and make great things happen for you. So, much of your leadership energy needs to be devoted towards building and nurturing a great team: from finding and recruiting people, through to shaping a collective culture, and investing in the development of individual people's talent and experience. Make that your first priority.

- **Network with purpose:** As well as a brilliant team to work alongside, you need a leadership network that is fizzing with brilliant mentors, peers, truth tellers, advocates and experts. However short on time you may feel, make sure to invest in cultivating contacts within and beyond your industry, in real life as well as social networks.

- **Provide clarity:** When it comes to making great things happen, make sure that everyone is on the same page from the outset, working towards the same strategic goals. Be transparent with information and ensure that you're constantly communicating, all of the time.

- **Navigate uncertainty:** At the same time, get ready to rip up your best-laid plans when circumstances change, as they inevitably will. Develop a culture of experimentation and innovation that will enable you to harness the opportunities that change brings.

Assignment: your *Stepping Up* plan

Reflect on the key insights

As part of investing in yourself, and as a fitting wrap-up to your investment in reading this book, think about how to turn the 5 Vs of this book into an actionable personal leadership development plan. Reflect back on the whole book, consider each of the key steps, and think first about the key takeaways for you – not everything will feel relevant or actionable, so choose the ideas that you, in your position today, are most excited about taking forward.

THE FIVE STEPS	MY KEY TAKEAWAY	MY NEXT STEP
1 **VISION:** Reset the rules		
2 **VALUES:** Make it matter		
3 **VELOCITY:** Invest in yourself		
4 **VOTES:** Invest in the team		
5 **VICTORIES:** Deliver brilliant results!		

Identify your *Stepping up* development Goals

Think about:

1. What is the goal?
2. Why?
3. Timescale
4. How will you know when the goal's been reached?

Step 1 Vision: reset the rules

MY DEVELOPMENT GOAL

. . . .

Timeline: What does resetting the rules look like in my role?	What steps will I take to get there?	What skills do I need to get there?	What does success look like?

Step 2 Values: Make it matter

MY DEVELOPMENT GOAL

. . . .

Timeline: What does making it matter look like in my role?	What steps will I take to get there?	What skills do I need to get there?	What does success look like?

Step 3 Velocity: invest in yourself
MY DEVELOPMENT GOAL

. . . .

Timeline: What does investing in myself look like in my role?	What steps will I take to get there?	What skills do I need to get there?	What does success look like?

Step 4 Votes: invest in the team
MY DEVELOPMENT GOAL

. . . .

Timeline: What does investing in the team look like in my role?	What steps will I take to get there?	What skills do I need to get there?	What does success look like?

Step 5 Victories: deliver brilliant results!
MY DEVELOPMENT GOAL

. . . .

Timeline: What does delivering brilliant results look like in my role?	What steps will I take to get there?	What skills do I need to get there?	What does success look like?

Be accountable

One last tip! We know this is a lot to think about but a thousand-mile journey starts with a single step. Monitor your progress over time. If you plan to adopt the *Stepping up* philosophy as your own leadership standard, you might find it helpful to openly share this ambition with your team and your trusted advisers. Go public about your desire to step up and become more purposeful. Ask your team or someone you trust to hold you to account to this new standard. Making your commitment public is an indication of how serious you are about living out these principles in day-to-day actions and decisions. This will be especially important in times of stress and challenge. We can all behave well when business is going well, but as we know the real test comes when you are under significant pressure.

The last word

Woohooo! You made it to the end! I hope you enjoyed reading about stepping up and what this looks and feels like in a new world of work, where the only certainty is change. You're on your way, dear leader, you're stepping up and the journey of your life is ahead of you.

Let's be honest, though, this book is just the preamble. The real journey starts now, with you, and with your next steps, and I can't wait to hear your stories and learn how you're stepping up to a more purposeful and empowering leadership role. If you'd like to share your own tips and tricks for #SteppingUp on Twitter, come and say hello at @sarahfwood and inspire others to take their next step! You'll find additional content and materials to download at https://unruly.co/steppingup. And don't forget, it's Ok to stumble too – that's all part of the journey. As my youngest daughter, Sunday (age 7), would say: 'You've got this'.

Sarah

Index